AF576507

International Development in Practice

List of Publications

Family in Contemporary Egypt (1984).

Reveal and Conceal: Dress in Contemporary Egypt (1986).

Within the Circle: Parents and Children in an Arab Village (1997).

Daughter of Damascus (1994).

Folktales of Syria (2004).

The Political Culture of Leadership in the United Arab Emirates (2007, 2010).

Simple Gestures: A Cultural Journey into the Middle East (2009).

Also:

Involving Communities: Participation in the Delivery of Education Programs (1998).

Starting Now: Strategies for Helping Girls Complete Primary (2000).

International Development in Practice

Education Assistance in Egypt, Pakistan, and Afghanistan

Andrea B. Rugh

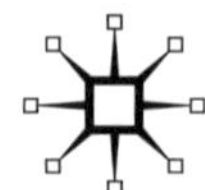

First published in 2012 by
PALGRAVE MACMILLAN® in the United States – a division of St. Martin's Press LLC, 175 Fifth Avenue, New York, NY 10010.

Where this book is distributed in the UK, Europe and the rest of the world, this is by Palgrave Macmillan, a division of Macmillan Publishers Limited, registered in England, company number 785998, of Houndmills, Basingstoke, Hampshire RG21 6XS.

Palgrave Macmillan is the global academic imprint of the above companies and has companies and representatives throughout the world.

ISBN 978–0–230–34017–6

Library of Congress Cataloging-in-Publication Data

Rugh, Andrea B.
International development in practice : education assistance in Egypt, Pakistan, and Afghanistan / Andrea B. Rugh.
p. cm.
Includes bibliographical references.
ISBN 978–0–230–34017–6 (alk. paper)
1. Education, Primary—Developing countries. 2. Education, Primary—Aims and objectives—Developing countries. 3. Education, Primary—Economic aspects—Developing countries. 4. Educational assistance—Developing countries. 5. Educational assistance—Egypt—Case studies. 6. Educational assistance—Pakistan—Case studies. 7. Educational assistance—Afghanistan—Case studies. I. Title.
LC2608.R84 2011
372.9172'4—dc23 2011025310

A catalogue record of the book is available from the British Library.

Design by MPS Limited, A Macmillan Company

First edition: January 2012

10 9 8 7 6 5 4 3 2 1

Printed in the United States of America.

To the committed development professionals both foreign and national who inspired me over the years

Contents

Tables

Preface

The aim of this book is to provide some real-life examples of donor-assisted primary education from the past several decades. It is not a "how to" book nor is it heavy on theory. Instead it describes what happened in actual projects and examines the social, political, and economic constraints under which development activities are designed and implemented. The case examples show that similar problems can arise in a variety of contexts, can be addressed in different ways, and produce different or similar results. The intention of the book is not to prescribe solutions but to sensitize readers to the opportunities and constraints that are an inevitable part of the assistance process.

University professors, trainers, and employers of consultants have long felt the need for studies on the practice of development in hopes that students and professionals can build on experience rather than repeat the mistakes of the past. The audience for the book is therefore graduate students, in-service professionals, and those in the general public interested in knowing how assistance work.

There are a number of reasons for the absence of literature on the practice of development. Foremost among them are the disincentives to providing candid assessments of projects. Most donors focus on success stories rather than descriptions of what went wrong or what corrections had to be made to overcome obstacles. Consequently, project staff usually only report failures when they are unavoidable "acts of nature" such as wars and other catastrophes "imposed" from the outside. The development community as a result is deprived of the lessons they might have learned from previous experiences.

This book describes the successes, failures, and weaknesses in three important education projects and in doing so reveals the difficulties educators face during program planning and implementation. The cases were chosen for several reasons. USAID has been a world leader in assistance to education over the past three decades, often setting the direction and approaches for interventions that others follow. Two of the cases (Egypt and Pakistan) are milestone cases for US support, while the third (Afghanistan) took place under the leadership of UNICEF with support from international NGOs.

The cases are loosely connected: (1) they are chronological and consequently able to benefit from the lessons of their predecessors; (2) they all started with the assumption that it was important to approach primary education comprehensively, and (3) the countries shared many of the same education problems. They were all low enrollment countries where rote forms of instruction prevailed, and where reforms of any kind were limited by the rigidity of bureaucratic structures.

Two other reasons for choosing these specific cases were, first that all had fairly discrete beginnings and ends so it was possible to follow them throughout the entire process and assess their overall impact. Second and undoubtedly more important was that the author had participated in all three, and could draw upon her experiences in making comparisons and drawing conclusions.

The cases shed light on the complicated relationships among local officials, outside experts, and donors, and raise important questions about "local participation"—what kind and by whom, and what roles consultants play. Other issues include the unintended consequences of change, unexpected obstacles that threaten progress, and questions about the sustainability of results.

Some of the most glaring problems encountered in these cases come from: (1) conflicting political pressures and the lack of political will to see reforms through, (2) failure to define objectives clearly, (3) different expectations about how reform should be implemented, (4) a lack of flexibility in bureaucracies to address problems, and (5) a failure to understand the incentive structures and constraints that motivate managers' behavior. The book explores all these issues.

The cases come with a perceptible bias about how education systems should work. This bias could be described as the belief (1) that the actual physical venue where schooling takes place is not essential to learning, (2) that there must be a clear definition of learning goals, and (3) that the method used to get to the goal is not as important as the fact that intended results are achieved. The beauty of this approach is that most countries already have the basic institutions to accomplish education goals so it should not be costly to make adjustments once there is the political will to do so. This theme runs throughout the book. When the projects turned out to be much more difficult to implement than this simple approach implies, it was usually because entrenched bureaucracies and vested interests obstructed or undermined change or the political will and leadership were lacking to see the projects through.

Some of the issues absent from the discussion are also important. These cases focus mostly on donor assistance to nationwide government systems with the goal of ultimately improving social indicators and education outcomes. They do not deal with the important but more limited efforts of NGOs and community-based organizations, except in the descriptions of Afghan refugee programs. The intent is not to denigrate these efforts but rather to limit the scope of the book. Another missing element is an exhaustive discussion of development ethics, again a matter of space because of the many issues that would have to be included.

One of the prevailing myths in development work is that good ideas will be adopted once their advantages become obvious, or the reverse, that bad ideas will be rejected once it is apparent they don't work. This myth has amazing staying power given the number of times it has proven false. Western experts too often rely on conventional wisdom about what works in their own countries, only to be disappointed when the ideas prove costly, unworkable, or a poor fit in the social and cultural environment of the recipient country. It is conventional wisdom, for example, to think learning works best in child-centered settings, and experts and political leaders alike continue to promote this idea even when countries' conditions are not favorable for such an approach. Often forgotten by outside experts is the underlying rationale for all education systems—to produce children with the skills expected of an educated adult in the local society. No matter how enlightened an outside idea may seem, it will have trouble finding roots in a society that has different expectations for the education of its children.

The book argues for reform based on solid evidence of impact. It is also a plea to use solid ideas of the past. It is sensible, for example, to try out innovations in limited environments before spreading them to the education system as a whole. It still makes sense to include formative assessment (monitoring) throughout the implementation process so impacts can be shaped and improved before it is too late or too costly to make changes. Simple, old-fashioned R and D (research and development) is largely missing in the modern haste to produce results. Project inputs based on untested assumptions invariably prove disappointing in the field.

Organization. The book is organized into six chapters. The first is an introductory chapter that reviews some issues in education assistances and explains the rationale for education reform in developing countries. The second gives examples of how the commonly found problems of education access, quality, and management have been addressed in various countries. The aim of these chapters is to review the issues requiring assistance and provide a repertory of options that have been used to solve them. The idea is to simulate the kinds of background knowledge experts should be bringing to the field.

The third through fifth chapters describe projects in three countries, showing the complex nature of factors impinging on reform and the ways consultants, local officials, and donors addressed them.

The sixth, conclusion chapter, compares the cases and draws lessons from them that may be useful in future development work. It describes how, within the limits of education budgets, there may be cost-effective ways to produce appropriate changes.

* * *

Over the past decade, the United States has introduced a number of far-reaching changes in the way it approaches assistance. Some of the most recent are as follows:

- Creating the Millennium Challenge Corporation in 2004 that complements other US development efforts by offering large grants directly to high-performing governments for their poverty-reduction programs;
- Increasing the number of US government agencies, in addition to USAID, including State, Health and Human Services (HHS), Treasury, Department of Defense (DOD), and Agriculture and Labor, engaged in their own foreign assistance efforts and adding staff for this purpose;
- Reconsidering the role that contractors and outside experts play in USAID assistance programs and recruiting significant numbers of direct-hire USAID staff to manage its programs. Over time USAID expects to become less dependent on private contractors and indefinite quantity contracts to manage its programs; and
- Drawing a distinction between long-term development projects and "Quick Impact Projects" (QIPs) designed for political visibility more than long-term results or systemic changes. Some donors for example find it easier to put large sums into visible school construction than less costly but also less visible quality improvements that may have a greater impact on learning.

All these changes suggest the timeliness of looking at what can be learned from the cases in this book.

Education is perhaps the most comprehensive and challenging of all development sectors. Not only does it affect other sectors but carries with it local sensitivities about what and how children should learn. Education bureaucracies exist within local power structures that may be reluctant to change or give up their areas of control. They have a past—whether colonial or indigenous—that is ignored at great peril and they are intimately bound up with the rules of culture and the norms of society. What happens in schools affects people's dreams for their children, and when programs go wrong their hopes are dashed. Getting it right benefits local society, the nation, and the international community. And yet in many parts of the developing and developed world education programs are failing. This is why we must make an effort to learn from previous experiences.

* * *

I would like to thank a number of people who have read portions of the manuscript and made useful comments. They include Mary Anderson, Molly Bang, Maureen Hsia, Jim Williams, and David Sprague. Others who have had a considerable influence on the ideas over the years are Mona Habib, Mouna Hashem, and Ellen van Kalmthout.

I am most of all grateful to Ann Van Dusen for testing one of the cases in her graduate class, and for her considerable editing advice and suggestions to improve the manuscript. She has been particularly helpful in contributing to sections related to USAID perceptions of events and suggesting questions and approaches for the study notes.

Finally I would like to acknowledge the work of the late Lillian Trager who had hoped to do a book on this subject but whose life was cut short before she had the time to do it.

* * *

Ultimately any inadvertent failures of memory or misperceptions are my responsibility alone. I have tried to represent these cases as factually as possible and whenever possible have relied on notes and documents produced at the time. A book like this however that attempts to be candid cannot fail to represent a point of view and I am well aware that colleagues who lived through these events with me may have different views of them.

Andrea B. Rugh

Chapter 1

Issues in Development

Introduction

There is little in the literature that describes the actual field practice of international development assistance. However two books written in the 1990s detailed the disappointing experiences of their authors. One writes about his time working on health care on the Red Sea Coast of Yemen.[1] He prefaces his mostly negative experiences with a description of why people do development. He says:

> Developmentalism is a beguiling creed, to be a developer of backward lands an attractive vocation. We all want to see ourselves as bearers of aid, rectifiers of past injustice. To be sent far away to a distant nation as a conveyer of progress can only make one feel good. It assuages the collective guilt induced by the legacy of our colonial predecessors. It invites admiration from those left behind. It boosts self-esteem. It is to regain certainty and purpose. . . . And to restore bracing faith in the goodness and charity of one's fellow men and women.[2]

The other author[3] writes of involvement in a World Bank project designed to transform the ruined economy of Equatorial Africa. The country required a detailed economic strategy of reform if the government was to obtain the financing it needed. The writer and his local counterparts worked hard to produce the strategy and gain approval for it. But the plan derailed when one of the key local participants was jailed for political reasons and the cooperating finance minister was sacked. The author writes:

> The Equatorial Guinea's leaders have not always known quite how to make the new strategy work—or in some cases whether they should really try. This ignorance and reluctance, though extreme, are in many ways prototypical and they raise general questions. How does one go about assessing an economy's strengths and weaknesses? How does one go about developing the institutions needed to make free markets work? And how can one help a recalcitrant, inefficient, sometimes corrupt government move forward? . . . What are the creative possibilities and the inherent limitations of such outside assistance? What are the tensions between aid and dependency, between benevolence and autonomy? And how would you have gone about the task . . . if you were me?[4]

These same questions could be asked for projects in a range of sectors. Although these two cases may have had more than their share of difficulties, anyone who has worked in the field will relate to their experiences. Even with brilliant designs, projects rarely anticipate all the hurdles that may derail them, and few end up meeting the full expectations of their designers. The projects mentioned above aimed to improve health care and alleviate economic problems, but the writers' experiences and cautions are also valid in countries where education projects are implemented. They make it even more imperative to describe projects as they actually occur rather than in a "dressed up" version that misrepresents reality. Future and current professionals need these unvarnished versions to prepare themselves to be better field workers, managers, and policy makers. It is unlikely they can deliver the best they are capable of, if they can't learn from the mistakes of those who came before them.

Issues

What Are Our Motivations in "Doing Development"?

Are they the ones described above? Do we as Americans do development from a charitable instinct, a sense of moral obligation, or guilt because we are a comparatively wealthy nation? Is it because we feel we have answers to difficult problems or in our boundless optimism as Americans, do we believe we can fix just about anything? Do we do it to improve the image of our country? Or because we believe our security depends on educated populations making good decisions about themselves and their relations with others? Is it because we worry that uneducated or undereducated populations are vulnerable to the distorted rhetoric of radical leaders? Does our country support development for purely political reasons or from an altruistic concern to see others prosper? The book can't answer these existential questions directly even though they are concerns every professional asks him or herself. In the end the reasons are probably a mixture of politics, hubris, generosity, personalities, and a genuine desire to improve the lot of others.

The Vocabulary of Development

Our ambivalence about the development process is seen in the changing way we describe development—what we are doing, how we are doing it, and who should be involved. Every few years a more politically correct way of describing the process becomes current, usually because the previous way seemed too patronizing, disrespectful, or downright insulting. Where do we from the "developed" or "advanced world" do our work—in "undeveloped," "underdeveloped," or "developing" nations? Do we do it in states that meet the Failed State Index's definitions of being "critical," "in danger," "borderline," "stable," or "most stable"? What do these terms mean? When, for example, does a developing country become a developed country? Is there only one route to development and are the "developed" countries the only acceptable model? This question is reminiscent of early anthropology that theorized a linear path toward civilization[5] where Western nations occupied the pinnacle of progress. A modern day version of this theory is Samuel Huntington's "The Clash of Civilizations" where one of the conditions he names for becoming developed is that developing nations adopt our core values, such as "punctuality" and a "strong work ethic." The implication is that if they don't adopt these values they will continue to muddle along in poverty and lack of enlightenment.

The vocabulary transitions go on. Are the "problems" we work to overcome "difficulties," "issues," "barriers," "obstacles," "constraints," "challenges," or "opportunities"? The slide in terminology leads increasingly to the implication that the constraints are surmountable and can be overcome. Are those we help "targets," "recipients," or "beneficiaries" of aid? Who should be involved—"governments," "local officials," "communities," "parents," "students," or "all stakeholders"? There is a subtle shift that takes people from being objects of assistance to being instrumental in their own reforms. How should we proceed—through existing local institutions, a reorganized bureaucracy, or by mobilizing certain groups to carry out the activities? Should we see the glass "half-full" and work up from the place where local people are, or see the glass "half-empty" and work down from the place we believe they should be? Which is more efficient, starting with grassroots communities or with high officials? How do we know when we have "succeeded" (or "failed")? What measures are appropriate for a "results-based" strategy? How enduring are highly visible short-term "Quick Impact Projects"[6] or should we be thinking more about long-term achievements? The terminology suggests the moral ambiguity developers feel when embarking on assistance.

Cultural Dissonances

Perhaps as much as any influence, culture shows up in development projects as one of the main issues. It is all the more pernicious when it is not recognized as such but rather labeled as "obstinacy," "failure of intellect," "backwardness," or "arrogance." Culture in this book is defined as a conceptual framework that shapes the way people see the world and their personal relationships in it. If we see the world through different cultural frameworks, how can we make sure we come to common understandings with our counterparts about development problems and their solutions? How do we know what to pay attention to or to ignore? What roles should local people play and how should they play them? What about the roles of foreigners? Although there is no one way of answering these questions they invariably confront the practitioner in the field. The greatest risk is in failing to understand the viewpoint of counterparts, since they can slow or altogether undermine activities. Another risk is in spending too much time with elites whose ideas are more likely to converge with the developer. Local persons at the grassroots level tend to be more highly immersed in the social and cultural expectations of their communities and may be more reliable informants.

An example of how international elites are more likely to understand one another is found in the international documents they sign on behalf of their governments. These documents include ones that describe children's rights, including the right to an education, as basic human values. Elites everywhere sign these documents even when local people in communally based societies would prefer to express these principles differently. Instead of talking about a child's rights, they would more likely see the provision of education services as a national obligation to the young. This is an important distinction that is often overlooked. A child may have the obligation to study hard once in school but is not necessarily seen as having an inherent right to go to school if he or she is needed to contribute to the welfare of the family. If asked to explain how rights fit into this view, a hypothetical parent might argue that the right naturally flows from the obligation. If parents fulfill their obligations the child receives an education; if not they are derelict in their duties and the negative consequence falls on the well-being of the group to which the parents and children belong.

Some argue that it is Western "individualistic" societies that focus so heavily on rights, while communally based societies instead emphasize members' loyalty and sense of obligation to their groups. Both sides may reinforce their arguments with religious references. The "individualistic" society may say that each person has a (God-given) right to the same opportunities and treatment as every other person. The "communally based" society says that every person has divinely prescribed obligations to every other person as revealed for example in the Koran and the practice of the Prophet Muhammad. In this latter example rights are created by human beings to protect against abusive people and governments, and therefore don't have the same power as divinely inspired obligations.[7]

One author explains[8] these different perceptions in terms of Eastern (communally based) and Western (individualistic) societies:

> Western customs, legal systems, and democracy look like a project to atomize society down to the level of individual economic units making autonomous decisions based on rational self-interest. Ultimately . . . this would pit every man, woman and child against every other. . . . What looks from one side like a campaign to secure greater rights for citizens irrespective of gender, looks from the other side, like powerful strangers inserting themselves into the private affairs of families and undercutting people's ability to maintain their communal selves as familial and tribal networks. In short, what looks from one side like empowering each individual looks, from the other side, like disempowering whole communities.[9]

This is a major difference of view that affects local receptivity to the designs of Western developers. Culture in effect influences every aspect of development when participants view the world in such different ways. In the cases dealt with in the chapters that follow, the reader will see that local participants were often thinking more about their obligations to their families and other groups while outsiders were trying to persuade them to provide services in an impersonal way for the good of the nation. Cultural dissonance explains much of what seems unexplainable in these cases.

The cultural differences are not confined just to communities with distinctly different ways of organizing. The United States and Europe for example sometimes provide assistance in demonstrably different ways. In a book on foreign aid to Morocco,[10] the author notes differences in the way these two groups provide support for democratic reforms. He says:

> The US approach draws on two aspects of the US experience. First the long history of decentralized control in the United States. . . . Few Americans can imagine a democracy that is not highly decentralized . . . In addition the United States is a highly individualistic society that places a premium on individual autonomy. Rights do not accrue to groups directly but . . . represent an agglomeration of the rights of individuals who belong to those groups. The European approach to aiding Morocco has tended to be centered less on the rights of individuals and directed more toward promoting change in the society at large . . . the state, on infrastructure, and on macroeconomic indicators . . . [and] to stress government-to-government dialogues as a path to promoting change rather than through extensive work energizing the grass roots. Such an approach is consistent with European norms which . . . tend to emphasize collective rights and societal prerogatives over the individual.[11]

The point here is that countries and individuals support the approaches to development they feel most comfortable with, the ones that lead to what they believe are the best outcomes. No one approach obviously trumps all others, but ignoring the way approaches derive from preconceptions risks failures later on.

Ethical Questions

The issues raised so far suggest the presence of a number of ethical questions related to the process of providing assistance. Some organizations spend considerable effort addressing these issues. UNICEF for example outlines the ethical concerns that are expected to inform all its activities. Its mandates call for staff to think carefully about the ethics of its approaches and the people it deals with—in the Afghan case, they are allowed to negotiate with the Taliban to promote the rights of vulnerable women and children as long as they adhere to "a principled approach" or at the very least they "did no harm" by their activity.

One can argue more generally "Who determines what is ethical?" Are we morally responsible because of our wealth, and if so to what extent?[12] Does our assistance on the other hand create a state of dependency, allowing recipient nations to avoid addressing their pressing financial and other problems? Can we legitimately require a nation to spend more of its budget on its school system before we make our own contribution? Should outsized loans be given to governments when it is clear they can never repay them and are simply pushing repayment into the future for another administration to deal with? Is it right to force reforms such as removal of subsidies on food and other items, onto the backs of the poor as a condition of international funding? Even if donor nations devote little time to these questions, they don't go away. Conflicting demands often give donors little room to choose those actions that make the most ethical sense. And as the cases will show, what looks to some as abandoning the "true" principles of development may be seen by others as meeting the needs of pragmatic political interest.

Participation and the Roles of Participants

We all know that the highest ideal of development is the full participation of local people. But that leaves considerable room for how they are involved and at what stage. Do they select the priority needs, design the approach, determine the goals and beneficiaries, or are they simply engaged in activities directed by outsiders hired by organizers and funders? Are there preferred roles for outsiders and insiders in an assistance program? Should communities be involved in shaping activities that affect them and if so, in what way? Are communities a necessary ingredient in supporting and sustaining education programs? Should scarce resources be spent on mobilizing and training villagers to support schools when those resources could be used elsewhere to provide more opportunities or better programs? Who should have the authority—local officials or donors—to decide the direction of project activities? How should consultants respond when they find abuses in the local system or in the use of assistance money? Should they become whistleblowers and compromise their ability to function effectively in the community?

Do consultants hired by donors have a first responsibility to achieve the donors' goals or is their ultimate obligation to the well-being of the beneficiaries? What happens when the consultant is hired by an international organization that in turn is hired by a donor, introducing a whole new layer of authority and accountability and potential for a conflict of priorities?

Much as we would like to think we mull carefully over these issues, it rarely happens in the heat of field work. "Why didn't you do such and such?" someone may ask. And the answer, more often than not, is that the pressures of field work caused us to take short cuts or fail to see all the implications of the way we were relating to our counterparts. Sometimes, what seemed the conventionally right way to do things proved not as effective as other approaches. One consultant for example "pushed" her counterparts hard in ways that were sometimes humiliating to them, but which in the end encouraged them to produce high-quality work. Her confidence in their ability to produce professional results overcame the humiliation, and she was universally loved in a way that was not true for more accommodating colleagues. These questions are not ones where the answers are immediately obvious.

The same is true for donors and those organizing development activities. They are caught between those who control the sources of money and can set the conditions for its use and consultants contracted to implement activities. People are human and each has his or her perspective on how the job should be done. Similarly, no matter how good a development design or how talented those who execute it there will be unexpected difficulties and unintended consequences that even the best of intentions can't overcome.

One frequent problem is that the designers of projects may not be the ones who implement them. The latter may not fully understand or accept the premises of the work, or worse, after arriving in the field find that a contracted activity simply doesn't make sense. Will the project officer require the activity anyway or will she/he allow modifications in the contract? Results can be wildly elusive and not always attainable in the form the contract states—projects are rarely entirely successful or completely a failure. The issue then is—can contracts be adjusted to produce the best results possible? Development is best approached with the idea that all the participants sincerely want to do what is right until irrefutably proven otherwise.

Why Education Assistance?

The considerations so far apply to virtually all development sectors. The question of whether or not to assist the education sector is one of the least controversial of assistance issues.[13] Along with health care—two of the fundamentals of a productive life—education is seen by most to be of universal importance, and decisions about supporting it often come down to the availability of funding, a donor's political interests, and where the need is greatest. It is no accident that the most important international development initiatives—the Millennium Goals and Education for All (EFA)—call for achieving universal basic education by the year 2015.

Research has shown that education provides the basic foundation for improvements in indicators that measure a country's development. Yet as international documents suggest many children still remain out of school, don't stay long enough to acquire functional literacy, or because of poor program quality don't acquire the skills they need to be productive adults. According to the EFA Monitoring Report (2010),[14] there were 72 million children out of school in 2007 and if conditions continue with no change there would still be 56 million children out of school in the target year 2015 when universal education should have been achieved. Of the out-of-school children, 54 percent are girls; and 759 million adults are still illiterate with two-thirds of them women.

The numbers remain significant despite considerable funding to increase enrollments in basic education[15] since 2000 when EFA targets were set in Dakar. The EFA identifies the marginalized groups as ones linked to wealth, gender, ethnicity, language, location, and disability. One study[16] showed that while these inequities exist overall, countries and regions tend to have specific patterns of where out-of-school children are located. The study implies that once these pockets of children are identified and the underlying reasons for their nonenrollment are known, resources can be narrowly focused on creating conditions that will encourage them to participate. In other words, generalized solutions may not work for these resisters who need special conditions to offset the reasons they remain out of school.

Although enjoying broad support, education assistance still raises issues that are potentially sensitive. Modern education is generally modeled on a "Western" system that sets out the parameters of what should be included (subject matter), how it should be provided (with sensitivity to gender issues, for example), and what kinds of methods ("child-centered") should be used. Where indigenous systems deviate from this model they are often criticized as being backward or ineffective or not providing all the skills children need.

By providing the main support for education, Western donors set the standard for how support should be provided and what stages of education should be a priority. They have tended to stress primary education and literacy programs believing these areas are the best way to achieve universal education. While that may be true, many recipient countries would prefer that more attention be given to higher education stages that lead to jobs. Focusing mainly on levels that achieve literacy ignores the fact that literacy still has little intrinsic value in rural villages where few reading materials exist and worse, in terms of dislocations, where even modest attainment of academic skills often alienates children from rural occupations.

Anyone who hesitates at the thought of education's downsides, however, has to remember that literacy is a cornerstone of a lot of other "goods" such as providing the foundation for higher levels of learning (we can't know who will flourish with opportunities), the possibility of expanded job possibilities, a healthier life style, and the likelihood that education will make children better parents later on. Even though education is not a sufficient requirement to realize these advantages, it often helps. The most convincing argument for supporting extended education is that although children may not be disadvantaged today by limited schooling (given high ratios of the highly educated unemployed), we cannot predict what children will face in the future. With that uncertainty it becomes important to prepare every child for the challenges he or she may face in the world of tomorrow.

There is another side beyond the presence or absence of benefits to individuals and their families. That is the undeniable benefit to nations of having an educated population. Studies have shown the advantages of an educated population in general and in particular the fact that girls' education is probably the single most important investment in international development. The benefits of educating girls fall into four broad categories:[17]

- Increasing income and productivity for individuals and nations;
- Smaller, healthier, better-educated families;

- Disease and HIV/AIDS prevention; and
- Women's empowerment.

Some of the specific findings that show how girls' education translates into national gains include the following:

- Educating a girl one year beyond the national average on average boosts her earning power between 10 and 20 percent.
- The estimated returns to female secondary enrollment are even higher at 15 to 25 percent.
- Increasing the proportion of women with secondary education by 1 percentage point boosts annual average per capita income growth by 0.3 percentage points.
- Doubling the proportion of women with secondary education reduces average fertility rates from 5.3 to 3.9 children per woman.
- Four added years of education per woman on average reduces the fertility rate of women by almost one child.
- An extra year of girls' education on average cuts infant mortality 5 to 10 percent.
- Educated women are roughly 50 percent more likely to immunize their children than uneducated mothers.
- A country's prosperity correlates with the parity between men and women in education. Pakistan has one of the largest gender gaps.[18]
- When half as many girls go to school as boys 21 infants per 1,000 die on average. That number is reduced as the gender gap narrows.
- Mother's education generally has more impact on children's education than father's education, and has significantly higher impact on daughters' enrollments.
- In India, a study showed that children of educated women study on average two more hours than children of uneducated women.
- Educated girls are less likely to contract HIV/AIDS.
- A Kenyan study showed that girls who stay in school are four times more likely to delay sexual activity.

- As women's share of income increases, more family money goes to food purchases and less to cigarettes and alcohol.
- In Bangladesh educated women were three times more likely to participate in political meetings than uneducated women.

These are just a few of the benefits that correlate with educating women. For the most part these benefits occur when groups of people extend their educations, making it worthwhile for governments and nations to invest generally in girls' education. Individuals of course do not benefit as predictably and therefore these national-level arguments are less compelling if personal reasons discourage children from attending. In other words, it is not a good advocacy argument for girls' education to tell parents that their daughters are likely to have fewer children if they stay in school longer. It is however a good argument when trying to get governments to allocate more money to the education sector.

Despite our considerable knowledge about the benefits of education assistance, the donor community possesses an uneven—some might say quixotic—record of responding to the challenges of providing a quality primary education for all. For example, it has had a tendency to focus narrowly on whatever conventional wisdom designates as "the magic bullet" of the moment: universal standards, curriculum development, teacher training, or leadership training. More often than not these strategies get imposed on contractors in "requests for proposals" and "earmarks" where they often leave little room for local needs and conditions to shape project designs. For better or worse, funding and the perceptions of funders ultimately play the significant role in determining the area for reform activities.

These are by no means all the issues that surround international assistance but they give enough of the flavor to see why the field is a kaleidoscope of conflicting ideas and arguments, and to show why the outcomes of projects are so difficult to predict in advance. The discussion of issues necessarily starts and stops with questions since there are no ready answers. Practitioners will inevitably have to find their own imperfect answers, if for no other reason than to move forward. Real progress, however, will only occur if the successes and failures of previous experience are documented in ways that allow us to make better use of our resources in the future.

Chapter 2

Meeting the Challenges of Education Assistance

Introduction

This chapter simulates, to the extent possible, the experiences of a field consultant who tries to stay abreast of research results and assistance efforts in various parts of the world. Space of course prohibits an exhaustive account of all that has been learned about education assistance, and these brief vignettes are therefore just a sample of the options used in various countries to solve education problems.[1] For convenience the vignettes and research findings are grouped into the three categories that emerge most frequently as the objects of education assistance:

- Increasing and extending education opportunities, or access;
- Improving the quality of academic programs; and
- Increasing local capacities to provide effective education services.

These categories overlap as they should—they are all highly interconnected—and consequently projects in one category may contribute insights to others. The project vignettes here come mostly from formal reports that tend to emphasize positive outcomes without describing the difficulties encountered during implementation. In the few cases where additional information is available to illuminate these issues, it has been included.

Each category is prefaced by a brief background summary of the problem to show that they are multifaceted and that projects rarely address them fully.

INCREASING ACCESS

Background

Girls have been a particular focus of international efforts to increase enrollments for the reasons summarized in the previous chapter. Educators often claim that once one generation of girls enrolls it will ensure that the next generation goes to school. Another claim is that initiatives directed at girls—whether they expand opportunities or improve program quality—will also benefit boys.

Schooling is considered accessible to children if they can overcome the physical, social, and economic barriers that prevent them from enrolling and staying in school until the end of basic education. In Egypt one study[2] showed that during the 1980s there had been a worsening of indicators such as the proportion of those entering grade one who completed the primary cycle, the average number of years it took to complete primary, and the proportion of primary graduates in the population.[3] The debate that ensued was concerned with whether the problem was caused by a lack of opportunities, family factors, or poor quality programs. The challenge for reformers is how to increase the desire for schooling among the poor, the rural, and girls where enrollments still lag.

Several studies have shown that lack of accessible facilities is probably the single most important factor limiting enrollments. The problem includes that facilities are too distant, too crowded, or substandard, or that it is too dangerous for children to reach school. Sometimes a school is used by a single group, such as boys or certain tribal or ethnic groups, and excludes others. Parents may consider the costs too high or see little value in education. There may be a shortage of teachers in remote areas, a lack of female teachers or of teachers qualified to teach certain subject matters. Countries have addressed these issues through policy changes, increasing infrastructure (schools), and increasing the numbers of qualified teachers. Sometimes incentives are used to increase the demand for education. Other initiatives mobilize community and private sector groups to support education. The sections below show some of the actions taken to increase participation.

Policy Reforms

Prior to funding of a comprehensive project in 1990, USAID and the Pakistani Government agreed that rural schools built under a new project would be designated single sex schools in the ratio of 60:40, girls to boys. After many of the schools had been built North West Frontier Province (NWFP) officials issued a new policy that declared all schools in their jurisdiction coed, thus effectively changing most of them to boys' schools when parents withdrew their daughters from environments where boys were present.

Malawi was having trouble retaining adolescent girls, in some cases because they were sexually harassed and became pregnant. Pregnant girls were expelled from school while the boys who were the fathers of the babies continued their studies. Officials formulated a gender-blind policy to deal with the problem. They expelled both the mother and the father and allowed them both to return to school after the baby was born.[4] A study however showed that most school principals either were not aware of the policy or did not enforce it. To make it better known, officials began discussing the policy on a radio station listened to by teachers.

Guinea also eliminated a discriminatory pregnancy policy and enacted a policy to appoint more female head teachers who it was hoped would be more sympathetic.

Increasing and Improving Infrastructure

A number of countries implemented construction components to increase the availability of opportunities. USAID funded 1,900 schools in Egypt during the 1980s that constituted 13 percent of the schools in that country. As a result, enrollments of targeted groups including rural children and especially girls rose significantly. In Pakistan in the 1990s and Afghanistan in the 2000s US-funded school construction was a major component of a multipronged education program.

In the 1990s the Guinean Government worked with NGOs and communities to build 1,500 classrooms in rural areas. A study in Kenya showed that increasing the number of schools had a more positive impact on enrollments of the poor than the rich, probably because there had been fewer spaces available to the poor.[5]

In Pakistan, the National Education Census (published in 2006) showed that 28 percent of the public educational institutions from primary to college level were without boundary walls, 41 percent without drinking water, 57 percent without electricity, and 7 percent without a building at all. These substandard conditions served as a deterrent to enrollments. Outside donors were able to make improvements in some facilities but because of limited funding were only able to address the problems in a few.

In Ghana when village committees were given grants to address the obstacles to girls' education, several chose to build latrines as the most important constraint on girls' enrollments, especially after puberty. Girls' persistence increased but the improvements did not help with the larger problem of low exam scores that prevented them from continuing into the next levels of education.

Increasing the Numbers of Qualified Teachers

In the face of inadequate numbers of rural teachers, Egypt gave preference in the 1980s to candidates for teacher training from remote rural areas. Pakistan relaxed rigid entry requirements based on exam scores that favored the entry of urban candidates to training institutions so that rural women would be given priority. It also built dorms where the women could stay during training. Ethiopia changed curriculum and admission policies at training institutes to encourage more female teachers. In the first year, female candidates increased by 65 percent.[6] The female teachers also received training and study tours to develop their leadership skills.

Encouraging Qualified Urban Women to Teach in Rural Areas

The World Bank thought urban women teachers might be willing to teach in villages of Pakistan if there were residential hostels nearby so they wouldn't have to commute long distances or stay with village families during the week. The Bank funded construction of 320 hostels in rural areas of Pakistan, but the effort was not successful. Single women refused to live in the hostels out of fear of compromising their reputations and married women had too many responsibilities at home during the week. The government tried other incentives such as increasing the salaries of urban teachers who would teach in rural areas, or letting a male family member live with them in the village.

Incentives to Encourage Enrollments

Community organizations in Egyptian villages administered a USAID-funded program of incentives to encourage at-risk girls to enroll, attend regularly, and show good learning results. The community groups identified the girls, provided them with school uniforms and supplies, and rewarded teachers who ensured they attended and that they and their classmates performed well on exams. Over several years, 188,810 scholarships were given out to 64,636 girls and to 11,222 boys who were the girls' younger siblings. When USAID support came to an end, the community organizations raised funds locally to continue the program.[7] The important aspect of this program was not only that it enrolled more girls but that teachers had to ensure their attendance and learning.

In Malawi a candidate for president won office on the basis of a platform of eliminating primary school fees and encouraging girls to continue by giving them stipends. In the first year girls' enrollments increased twice as much as boys. Difficulties arose however when children overwhelmed primary schools that were not prepared with teachers, space, or textbooks to cope with so many. The costs of "free" schooling and stipends were difficult for the government to sustain, and an academic program that had been quite good, deteriorated under the weight of the influx.[8]

Benin also eliminated school fees with the result that girls' enrollments increased by 30 percent.[9] Incentives for girls' enrollments can also be nonmonetary, such as mentoring by educated, working women who serve as role models or, as in Malawi, displaying calendars that feature prominent women. In Morocco rural girls who wanted to continue to middle and secondary levels were given stipends to pay for their room and board with relatives in towns where these levels were available. The girls attended sponsored study groups in the evening to make sure they kept up with their studies.

Free Textbooks, Uniforms

A study in Kenya comparing schools where children received free textbooks with schools where they did not showed significantly higher enrollments, better attendance, and reduced dropout rates but not better test scores in the experimental schools.[10] Free textbooks given out during trials of new materials in Pakistan unexpectedly stimulated increases in enrollments in the early grades (see Pakistan case study below).

Sensitization, Advocacy Campaigns

In the early 1990s Guinea conducted national and village campaigns to sensitize communities to the importance of girls' education through discussion and dialogue. By the end of the decade girls' enrollments doubled as a result of this and other actions. A number of countries in Latin America including Guatemala have used media campaigns to encourage girls' enrollments. Some private businesses sponsored ads on their product containers to promote girls' education.

Malawi sent a troupe of university students called Theater for Development to spend a week each in villages where girls' enrollments were low. Troupe members participated in daily life and tried to understand attitudes toward girls' education. Each evening they discussed what they learned and near the end of their visit performed lively dramas for the village that countered negative attitudes and constraints on girls' education. The Ministry of Education (MOE) also established a Gender Unit to make the curriculum more gender-neutral, to implement reform policies, and to provide incentives for girls to enroll and continue in school. These and other actions saw a 71 percent increase in girls' enrollments in Malawi and eventually girls outnumbered boys in primary school.[11]

A project in Uttar Pradesh, India, developed a training module that helped teachers identify and eliminate gender bias in their classrooms to increase girls' participation. In Ethiopia workshops were conducted to sensitize students to gender issues and provide them counseling and support services.

Early Childhood Education

India set up preschool programs in poor neighborhoods where, in addition to participating in prelearning activities, children received food and health care. The aim was to accustom parents to the idea of regularly bringing children to school and helping them make the transition into first grade. The program also relieved older children from taking care of younger siblings so they could attend school.

Multisectoral Advocacy

Between March 1999 and July 2002 the SAGE[12] project helped organize broad-based, multisectoral constituencies—including the media, community-based organizations (CBOs), and political, religious, ethnic, and business leaders—to encourage the participation of girls in five countries: Guinea, Mali, Ghana, El Salvador, and the Democratic Republic of the Congo. SAGE provided local partners with technical services to advocate for girls' education, convened conferences, and conducted studies to show how nontraditional partners might support girls' education. Evaluations concluded that multisectoral approaches are most effective when there is dynamic local leadership to solve problems, good coordination and communication among the partners, and when the approaches are kept flexible. Participants, for example, in villages, would identify obstacles to girls' education and with the help of organizing partners (who often funded the activities) would implement them. The projects included such initiatives as latrines, building classrooms, mentoring, girls' clubs, and others. The report cautioned that before expanding this approach, careful consideration should be given to the trade-offs, on one side, the significant effort that goes into mobilizing nongovernmental groups against alternative investments in education that might be a more efficient use of resources.[13]

More Attractive, Relevant Programs

In Latin America, *Fe y Alegria* (a private NGO run by Jesuits with teachers paid by the government) implemented a program designed to make schools more effective and relevant so they would attract at-risk children. The program established centers for formal and nonformal classes and for community activities involving parents. Learning materials were based on government objectives but with content locally determined. Teachers had responsibility for making sure children learned, and their innovative ideas were transmitted to other centers in the network. Eventually 12 countries adopted the program. *Fe y Alegria* attracted and retained more students than conventional schools, while student performance remained comparable.[14]

Mobilizing Community Support

Many education projects now require a community participation component by their funders. However, considerable debate surrounds the question of whether or not community support is a cost-effective way to achieve education goals. One study[15] that reviewed several projects with a substantial community participation component concluded that while participation helped increase enrollments, especially of girls, it did not substantially improve the quality of the program as measured by exam scores. The study further questioned whether mobilizing communities was worth the time and resources that would be taken from other program needs.

Another study looked at community involvement in reading programs in India where one group of parents were told in meetings about how Village Education Committees worked and how through them parents could make improvements in the education program. The second group was given the same treatment but also learned how children would be evaluated on report cards in their local schools. The third group was chosen from volunteers who attended several days of demonstrations of techniques to help children read. Those who expressed interest were given more training and told they could organize reading groups on their own. The third group was the only one of the three to improve children's reading but the improvements didn't last. The author concluded:

> Whatever the explanation, it seems clear that the current faith in participation as a panacea for the problems of service delivery is unwarranted. It is possible that it can be made to work on a more systematic basis, but it would take a lot of patience and experimentation to get there.[16]

Studies in Ghana[17] showed that villagers were most active in mobilizing support—often labor and financing—at a point when schools were being established but that support later dwindled as did attendance at PTAs until most ceased to exist. The reasons given for these outcomes included that

PTAs were given supportive rather than directive roles in the management of schools and became tired of recurring economic burdens, that school staff were accountable to superiors and could not be sanctioned by parents for poor teaching or poor attendance, and that parents ultimately became disenchanted with the increasing costs and decreasing benefits of education.[18]

In Tanzania, a Community Education Fund was established to match community funds raised to improve schools. The amount was based on the relative economic level of the community as measured by graded school fees with more being given to poorer communities. To participate, a number of actions were required including approval of designs and permits for improvements, a bank account, and financial record-keeping. The pilot study showed that substantial funds were collected, but there was a question of whether communities spent them on priority needs (they tended to spend them on buildings rather than textbooks, teacher supplies, or inputs to improve quality) and whether the project stimulated long-term community responsibility.[19]

Nonformal Programs

A number of countries provide literacy and nonformal courses for out-of-school children and adults. Between 1994 and 1997 USAID partnered with NGOs to provide literacy programs to 425,000 Nepalese women. Observation of the classes suggests that few participants actually attain functional literacy, but the classes served the useful purpose of transmitting health and other information. They also give women who learn a few basics and the ability to sign their name a feeling of self-worth that sometimes translates into "educated behavior" such as immunizing their children and sending them to school, and using healthier hygiene practices. In general the most successful students in literacy classes tend to be girls and women before they marry and married women no longer having to care for young children. Others were either too busy or not able to adapt well to lessons, especially when they had never attended school before.[20]

Pakistan established a number of schools to reach out-of-school children including "mosque schools" where government teachers provided instruction in language arts, and math, and the imam was paid to give religious instruction. Another system, the Nai-Roshni ("drop-in") schools, provided instruction for those too old to enter school and those who had dropped out. Both systems were eventually halted because of hostility from the education hierarchy to their "poor quality."

A project in Egypt for out-of-school girls called "New Horizons" gathered field workers from social service NGOs and other Egyptian organizations to write life skills manuals appropriate for use in their social programs. The topics were identified through discussions with villagers and included such subjects as reproductive health, female genital cutting, and virginity tests as well as a range of health, first aid, household economic issues, income producing, and legal issues. Girls learned about their rights under the Egyptian constitution including their right to an education. The information was embedded in lively role-playing and drama productions and the course was so popular that in-school children asked to attend. Later materials were modified for youth groups. Over 100,000 children took part in this training. The training followed a sequence of steps that moved through "less sensitive" topics in the trainers' manual, on to reproductive health topics for girls over the age of eight. After completing these lessons the girl could take literacy courses and eventually courses in accounting and starting a small business. The success of this project was attributed to the fact that the recruited writers who prepared the materials would use them in their own classes, the local interest in the topics, and the organizers obtaining permission from community councils to teach the sensitive issues.[21]

IMPROVING QUALITY

Background

It has taken time for assistance agencies to recognize the importance of quality. Focusing narrowly on enrolments has largely been based on the assumption that children will learn basic skills despite weak programs. However, that has not always proved true in practice. Children are less likely to be attracted to schooling programs, and may drop out early without attaining functional skills if the program is of poor quality. If they fail exams parents may not encourage them to continue. As usual these eventualities tend to affect girls more than boys.

A major problem has been that "quality" is hard to define. It has been variously defined as certain kinds of existing measures (pass rates, exam results, progression rates), as classroom environments, teacher characteristics and teaching methods, or as certain kinds of inputs (class size, libraries, teaching kits, and availability of instructional materials). Often improving quality has meant developing inputs like curriculum and instructional materials that are sensitive in the local context. As a result of these complexities, outside donors rather than addressing academic programs comprehensively have tended to focus on limited aspects of problems like teachers training while leaving other elements like testing, instructional materials development, and research and development untouched.

Studies have shown overall that in the 1980s and 1990s quality as measured in test scores and repetition rates worsened in most African countries, in several Arab countries, and Southwest Asia. The decline has been attributed to increasing numbers of children flooding the schools, the hiring of less well-trained and academically prepared teachers, and less selective student admissions, among other factors. In Egypt, school quality as measured by test scores, which had never been high, deteriorated during the 1980s.[22] Studies differed on where to place the blame—on family factors and deteriorating economic conditions, or teacher characteristics, teaching practices, and schooling environment.[23] One study blamed poor learning outcomes mainly on low attendance levels.

We have not looked at funding in this section on quality. One researcher claims that "in the case of education, rigorous, randomized evaluations have found little evidence that more resources on their own, with no changes to the way education is delivered, can improve test scores."[24]

Comprehensive Approaches to Improving Quality

The Bangladesh Rural Advancement Committee (BRAC) is perhaps the best known and most imitated model to address the education needs of children in poor communities comprehensively. BRAC schools are of two types: a three-year nonformal primary program (NFPE) for eight- to ten-year olds and a two-year program for eleven- to fourteen-year olds. The aim of these schools is to reach children who would not otherwise go to school and teach them basic literacy and numeracy in this shortened program. Of the students, 70 percent are girls and 90 percent of those who enter grade one graduate. A large proportion go on to government schools at grade four or higher. The second type of BRAC school is a two-year program for 11- to 16-year olds who have dropped out of government primary schools and don't plan to return. The schools are small (roughly 30 students), the teachers have grade nine diplomas or higher, are local, and are hired on contract. The school is in session 2 hours a day, 6 days a week, 268 days a year and children must attend regularly. Parents attend monthly meetings. The teaching approach is supposed to be child-centered and activity-based but traditional methods tend to dominate. The curriculum has been improved several times. Subjects are Bangla, social science, and math, and in the last year, English. A continuous assessment system is used. Children who complete the BRAC program perform as well or better than children in the government schools. Roughly 50 percent achieve functional literacy, much higher than the children of the same level in the government system. However, they often have difficulty making the transition into the government system where the instructional methods are different and many drop out after a year or two.

Two Save the Children (STC) programs in Mali (seventy-five schools) and Malawi (eight schools) modeled on the BRAC approach, are aimed at improving schooling quality. They differ from government schools in that teachers are selected from the community and usually have no more than primary certificates, instruction is in the local language, and the curriculum is scaled down and made more relevant. Classes are small; teachers have considerable supervision; there are in-service teacher training, free books, and supplies; and the community is involved. In both countries STC children perform on exams as well or better than children in the government schools, their repetition and dropout rates are lower, and they more often go on to higher stages.[25] The characteristics of the experimental and government schools unfortunately were too different to make valid comparisons of their relative effectiveness. One important consideration however was that STC schools were provided with considerable outside funding that could not be sustained at these levels after the end of the project.[26]

UNICEF also patterned its community schools in Pakistan and Egypt on the BRAC model. These schools were owned by communities rather than the government. In Egypt in 1996 USAID supported more than 110 community schools with 3,000 students of which 70 percent were girls and they were planning 1,000 more. These schools based on more child-centered approaches sometimes had difficulty preparing and getting children into the next stages of government schools where learning methods and goals differed.

Inputs to Raise Test Scores

In Kenya, free textbooks were given to children in one set of schools and the impact was compared with a control set of schools that did not receive them. Although the free books increased enrollments, overall they did not increase test scores. But further analysis showed scores rose in schools where enrollments increased the least and fell in schools where enrollments increased the most, which may have been due to fewer teacher and inputs per pupil in schools with higher enrollments. Holding other factors constant the author concluded that the books were more cost-effective in raising test scores than reducing class size.[27]

Also in Kenya, a study[28] compared increases in resources alone (changes in pupil-teacher ratios from 82 to 43 per teacher on average) to two frequently advocated changes in the organization of teaching: the use of locally hired teachers on short contracts and the involvement of parents in the management of schools. It found that if there were no other change, teachers simply expended less effort and test scores did not improve significantly. However students who were taught by contract teachers experienced significant improvement in test scores, as did those in schools where school committees were given training in how to improve performance. The study found that reducing class size alone was not a key to improving school quality without making changes in the school environment itself to promote better learning. The better performance of contract teachers may have been due to a better choice of teachers or due to the incentives of becoming tenured if the teacher performed well. The parent committee had an impact on student performance probably because they monitored teacher attendance. The author attributed this to the fact that parents were given a concrete agenda of what to do.[29] This study shows as have others that increasing resources alone may not be sufficient to improve school quality without changes in incentives or in the organization of the teaching environment.

Language of Instruction

The use of foreign languages as the medium of instruction has been identified as one of the most important obstacles to learning in African nations[30] as well as in other parts of the world. Kenya, Ghana, Haiti, Malawi, Mali, Pakistan, and some parts of Afghanistan all face this problem. In a few countries the early curriculum starts in a local language before switching to the official foreign language. Often teachers themselves do not speak the foreign language well enough to teach it. In Kenya, Pakistan, and a number of other countries, Interactive Radio Instruction has been introduced to teach foreign languages with a good measure of success. In Guatemala, where there have been difficulties enrolling Mayans, books were produced in four Mayan languages, with posters and Mayan designs. In roughly five years the enrollment of Mayans in the bilingual schools increased 34 percent compared to 11 percent in Spanish language schools, and girls' participation in the upper grades increased 36 and 43 percent in 1993 and 1996.[31]

School and Classroom Characteristics

Although most studies of school characteristics show that pupil-teacher ratios up to a certain level have little effect on test scores, a study in South Africa showed that reducing the number of children from 40 to 30 increased educational attainment by a third of a year. The study claimed this impact would be extended into the next generation since length of parents' education correlates with children's enrollment and attainment. However, the author concluded that there were too many other contributing factors to recommend this as a solid policy option.[32]

Teacher Training

Assistance frequently focuses on teacher training to improve program quality. Almost any assistance effort that addresses "quality" has a training component, usually in the form of in-service workshops. *Escuela Nueva* and the many countries in which it is implemented rely on workshops that train teachers in how to develop and implement *Escuela Nueva*'s special features. Others including Pakistan, Afghanistan, Ethiopia, Kenya, Malawi, Mali, Pakistan, Nepal, and many others have project-supported teacher training programs. Workshops are popular because they are short in duration, cover a number of participants, and are presumed to be a way of broadening teachers' understanding of new methods and approaches, and improving student learning. The weakness of many training efforts is that teachers often can't translate the new ideas into existing classroom contexts since instructional materials and exams don't reward the kind of learning they promote, and rarely is their impact on learning ever assessed.

Teacher Preparation and Knowledge

Studies in two African countries—Togo and Sierra Leone—show that students performed poorly on math and science exams. They placed blame for these results on teachers' insufficient academic and professional training in these areas. In Pakistan the NWFP curriculum unit prepared booklets on primary school concepts in math and language arts and encouraged teacher training institutes to improve teachers' subject content knowledge (studies showed teachers performed at about the same low level as fifth graders on primary leaving exams). The institutes refused since their federally mandated curriculum charged them with teaching instructional methods and not subject matter.

Programmed Learning

The Philippines established an innovative learning program called Instructional Management by Parents, Communities, and Teachers (IMPACT) in the 1970s. The program consisted of learning modules based on skill objectives that children could complete at their own pace. Once they demonstrated mastery of a module they could move on to the next. The program used parent volunteers and peer teachers (older children teaching younger children) so that very little formal instruction was required of teachers and instead they acted as managers and monitors of learning. On tests, children in IMPACT schools achieved as high or higher scores than those in conventional schools, but many parents were unhappy with such an unconventional model and ultimately the program was dropped.[33]

Teacher-Developed Materials

In Colombia (and other countries of Latin America), USAID has supported the well-known *Escuela Nueva* (see above) since 1975. The program was intended to increase the participation of rural children and improve the quality and relevance of education programs. Teachers were trained to be facilitators of education and provide out-reach to communities. They convened periodically in workshops to develop materials for their own classrooms based on government curriculum objectives but using content more relevant to the local environment. The teachers used the local community to provide historical lore, folk practices, labor, and for help in tutoring children. The program in its initial stages was effective in encouraging community participation and improving school outcomes. In Columbia the number of schools participating increased from 500 to 20,000 schools in the first three years, with enrollment increases of 81 percent for girls and 78 percent for boys. Students typically exceeded achievement in conventional schools.[34] When the program was expanded to the national level and to other countries of Central and South America however it proved less effective. Among the reasons were that it was inconsistently implemented, met resistance from traditional educators, was insufficiently resourced, and depended almost entirely on the initiative of already overworked teachers.[35]

Child-Centered Approaches

Over a number of years the Aga Khan foundation has supported child-centered teaching techniques to improve critical-thinking skills and learning. Teachers learn the techniques in workshops and then are supported by classroom coaches (daily for four months) and appropriate instructional materials. The approach was phased into schools in Kenya over a six-year period. The test scores were mixed and the "child-centered teaching behaviors . . . did not seem to have a positive influence on test scores."[36] The long-term use of teaching coaches makes the approach very costly and labor intensive.

Multigrade Instruction

Most government schools and training are geared to the single-class model, which makes it difficult in rural schools to address the special requirements of multigrade schools. In Guatemala in the late 1990s, half of all rural schools were multigrade "one-room schools." They used a Neuva Escuela Unitaria (NEU) model that included collaborative learning, peer-group teaching, self-instructional guides, student government and community outreach. Teachers were trained in how to deal with multigrade classes. Dropout rates decreased by 12 percent over conventional rural schools and children were twice as likely to progress a grade each year. NEU students also achieved scores in reading and mathematics tests at the same rates as students in conventional schools. Community schools in Egypt use a similar multigrade child-centered approach.

Instructional Time

In Pakistan, children in multigrade classes frequently performed less well on exams than children in single-grade classes. A small study determined that the multigrade students were spending significantly less time engaged in academic tasks than students in single-grade classes. The study recommended "contingent" tasks, so that when teachers were occupied with other class levels, the unattended students were assigned tasks with concrete evidence of their work—so teachers could be certain the students engaged in learning tasks while they were otherwise occupied (previously students memorized work or read).

Instructional Materials

In Pakistan, the National Education Census (published in 2006) showed a lack of educational resource materials to facilitate children's learning. Teachers in Pakistan often lacked textbooks or a copy of the curriculum and many in rural areas didn't have maps or posters to illustrate class work. A teaching kit supplied to Pakistani teachers in the mid-seventies had never been updated and in many cases was not used. Library books, if they existed, stayed locked in cupboards to prevent them from being damaged. In Yemen textbooks and other materials often came several months into the school year, leaving teachers scrambling to organize their teaching until they arrived.

More Relevant Programs

In the 1980s Egypt experimented with teaching primary students prevocational skills in primary schools but these courses turned out to be difficult to implement and costly, and parents reacted negatively to them (see Egypt case) and they were abandoned.

In Mali rural parents claimed they kept children home because schools didn't teach them skills that were relevant. Meetings with parents discovered that they wanted their children to learn practical skills like carpentry and mechanics where they could earn an income. The budget of the Malian Government however was unable to support such costly courses. After discussions, parents agreed that reading and math skills would also be useful for their children especially if accompanied by information about illness prevention, health, nutrition, first aid, environment, and other life skills. Ministry staff attended workshops and wrote roughly 100 units of life skills materials around stories of a village girl who solved village problems (much like the Meena advocacy stories in India). The Ministry developers later decided to incorporate the materials into the textbooks when they were rewritten.

Interactive Radio Instruction (IRI)

One of the major issues in trying to achieve quality programming is the uneven implementation of the curriculum. One way to ensure more consistent program quality is through IRI. IRI is often used (see above) in situations where instruction is poor, teachers are not qualified to teach a certain subject, or where teachers are not available. Sometimes, as when a foreign language is used in instruction, children must develop fluency quickly in order to learn other subjects. The system has been used in more than 18 countries to teach subjects as varied as math, science, English, Spanish, Portuguese, environmental education, early childhood development, and adult basic education. The programs are designed by local specialists to make them interesting for the learners and to meet the specific learning objectives of the country. The lessons are transmitted through radios or audio cassettes. An adult, usually the classroom teacher, facilitates the session wherein a radio teacher directs the activities and in timed pauses the class responds. IRI learning has repeatedly proven effective—students show gains over control groups and the gains grow over time. The program is also highly competitive in terms of costs compared to alternative strategies. Although repeatedly proven effective however these programs often face political opposition or simply people's old-fashioned beliefs about how instruction should take place.[37]

Second Chance Education Through Radio

Honduras had high rates of enrollments and no gender gap, but had high dropout and repetition rates because of poor academic performance. To combat these problems the government instituted radio learning programs to improve primary level math and to provide an accelerated program so adults could earn the equivalent of a primary diploma. Both were successful programs but the math program lost its funding.[38]

Increasing Capacity

Background

Assistance efforts to improve capacity are often less visible, and more often a part of ongoing projects focused on expanding schooling opportunities and improving quality. One could argue that local participation in any of the projects above is a kind of hands-on training for those involved. However, this experience may not pay off if the number of trained participants is limited, there is significant turnover of staff, or if the skills are not called for again after a program loses its funding. Most education bureaucracies in the developing world focus on administering school systems—admitting students, hiring and paying teachers, and implementing exams—instead of managing education programs, which involves planning, analysis, identifying problems and solving them, assessing options and alternatives and figuring out the most cost-effective ways to use chronically short resources.

Other problems of capacity include a lack of tools to adequately make decisions—in many countries, record-keeping is ineffective; data-collection methods and processing are weak; and staff don't have the skills to analyze information effectively. Most education bureaucracies also lack the research capacity to solve problems and continue to enforce inflexible policies that prevent reform. Political will is also a major factor in whether reforms take place and are sustained.

Political Will

Political will can be a factor at all levels of the education system from a political leader at the top of the government, to a Minister in charge of education, to officials and educators at other levels, to school principals, and even to community leaders. Studies in Egyptian rural areas for example found that when a village had high levels of enrollment over a long period, there was almost always a mayor or respected individual who had taken a special interest in the school and made sure village children attended.

Oman's ruler Sultan Qaboos came to power in 1970 after overthrowing his father in a coup. At the time there were three boys' schools with 909 students. As a result of strong pressure from the Sultan, 20 years later there were 703 primary and secondary schools with almost 300,000 students, including 95 percent of the age cohort of girls. Girls make up 46 percent of primary and 51 percent of secondary enrollments. Oman is not a wealthy country so this extraordinary achievement meant the country made sacrifices in other areas.[39]

Education ministers in a number of countries have had outstanding impacts on their education systems. One was Aicha Bah Diallo, Minister of Education for Guinea (1989–1996). She created the Declaration of Education Policy in 1989 that increased the budget for education to 20 percent with most of the money going to the primary level. Her goal was to increase enrollments from 28 to 53 percent of age-appropriate children in a decade and reduce the disparities between gender and other groups. She also recruited and trained teachers and added classrooms to keep up with these increases. After six years, overall primary enrollments increased 68 percent, including girls' enrollments that increased 60 percent, and rural girls' rates that increased 92 percent. The repetition rate decreased by 6 percent.[40]

Financing Education

The amount a developing country invests in its education sector often indicates its seriousness about reform. The UN recommends a minimum of 4 percent of GNP. Underfunding of basic education has been addressed in a number of ways: by allocating more of a country's budget to education, by redistributing local resources so more are focused on the primary level (in many countries it is heavily weighted toward higher stages), and by directing more international support away from tertiary and vocational training (that is better paid for by the private sector and parents) to basic education. Up until now, households bear a disproportionate share of shortfalls in basic education.

Assistance agencies may require as a condition for their support that a developing country increase its education budget. USAID encouraged Ethiopia for example to increase its education budget, which it did by 8 percent. Guinea increased its investment in education to 17 percent of GNP in the late 1990s and implemented a program where Guinean communities contributed 25 percent of school construction costs.

How funds are allocated can also have an impact on education goals. In Pakistan, the province of Balochistan pays for textbooks for rural children while NWFP does not although indications suggest that this policy change alone might increase rural enrollments significantly.

A UNESCO-UNDP report in Africa found that the crisis in education financing was largely due to the state's monopoly and tight control over the school system. This control discouraged private support for alternative programs and relied on parents for school fees without giving them ownership of the outcomes.[41]

Cost-Efficiencies

Another factor that contributes to budget shortages is the poor administration of existing resources. A model in this respect is the management system used by BRAC, which carefully identifies need, plans costs of opening new schools, and ensures the quality of programs, all at minimum cost. When problems are identified in any component of its program, discussions are held to seek a solution and then the solution is implemented in limited trials and if found effective, brought to scale in the program as a whole.[42]

In countries (such as Afghanistan) that insist upon sex-segregated spaces for education, it becomes difficult to provide two schools in every village, but it might be possible to have a shift system using the same building or separating school entrances and dividing the school so both sexes could attend at the same time. Sometimes the education department—for example, in Balochistan—has two parallel bureaucracies, one to administer girls' schools and one for boys' schools.

A study in Burkina Faso showed that poor coordination and management of education finances, made it difficult to appeal for more funding.[43]

Planning

The lack of effective planning in many countries is at least partly due to the absence of tools such as rigorous data collections, their management, and analytical capacities to achieve efficiencies. Missing also is a felt need to go beyond rudimentary statistics about teacher, student, and school numbers, or to accept the conclusions of studies and evidence. Egypt and Pakistan have improved their capacities to collect and analyze data with outside assistance, but have been slower to use the data in planning as effectively as they could have.

Devolving Decision-Making Authority

One reason bureaucracies are so slow to solve their education problems is that decision making has become a personalized affair involving limited numbers of officials in the capital city. As a consequence no one has full authority at the local level to work out problems where they are likely to occur. Decentralization is often recommended as a way to solve this problem by devolving certain kinds of authority to local education offices. Pakistan, Egypt, and other countries have implemented this idea in full or in part. This has involved variously moving certain types of decision-making power from the federal levels to regional levels and from there to district and even to school levels. In Ethiopia for example an effort is being made to move a great deal of the decision making to school-based management. Other countries have also assigned quality monitoring and accountability functions to school principals, and sometimes to village education committees.

Management

In Guinea USAID and the World Bank supported a National Education Policy frame work and strategy (PASE) that was designed to improve the organizational capacity to improve the quality of schooling. As a result of the technical support, repetition rates in Guinea decreased by 6 percent over two years.

A USAID-funded Girls' and Women's Initiative (GWE, called Girls Education Activity (GEA) in some countries) operated in six countries in the 1990s. In Morocco the goal was to increase the institutional and management capacity of NGOs to work in girls' education, to involve civil society and particularly the private sector in creating awareness campaigns about the need for girls' education. Participants believed the project provided a "robust option for improving the education of girls" and "a change in the climate of public dialogue about girls' education."[44]

In Pakistan, the Community Support Project (CSP) in Balochistan mobilized communities to support schools in villages where no schools existed. Community members verified the academic skills of a potential teacher (with at least an eighth grade education) through testing, and then she was trained in a "crash mobile course." After graduation the government gave her textbooks for a class she organized. When it became clear the community was taking responsibility for seeing that children and teacher attended regularly, the government built a school and supported the teacher's salary. The village committee would continue to supervise the school by monitoring the attendance of teachers and students and delivering textbooks and other supplies. In a 5-year period 200 girls' schools of this type were established in Balochistan with a doubling of the girls' enrolled in their areas.[45]

Establishing Units to Highlight Specific Issues

Because of the high rates of HIV infections and deaths among males in Malawi, it became imperative to attract more rural girls to school so they could help support their families in the future. The Malawi Institute of Education established a Gender Appropriate Curriculum (GAC) Unit to deal with girls' and women's issues. Its responsibility included sensitivity training for officials, school staff, and communities and review of all new curriculum materials for gender imbalances. The staff found they had to be proactive or other groups charged with curriculum development and training would ignore the requirement that they consult with the GAC Unit.

In Pakistan, when NWFP departments responsible for curriculum and testing were located at a distance from the provincial headquarters and could not coordinate their activities, branch units were established nearby to deal with these issues.

Final Word

The projects described in this chapter are a small sample of the kinds of activities implemented around the world to increase enrollments and improve quality and capacity in the education sector. The main focus of these particular efforts is the primary level and numerically the aim is most often to increase the enrollment of girls. This reflects the reality of assistance in the past two decades.

Space is too limited to provide all the interesting details of these projects—some are addressed in more depth in the case studies that follow. Most of the descriptions above come from project and donor reports, which are notable for not mentioning constraints or revealing where projects failed to meet expectations. Running through the reports however are some consistent themes. First, many assume that specific impacts will automatically result from certain actions, even though few if any efforts are made to assess the correctness of these assumptions. Second, rarely if ever do implementers compare the effectiveness of possible alternatives, or determine how a chosen option compares in cost with maintaining the status quo. We hear repeatedly that reforms are a success if their results are the same as those in the conventional system. Even granting that experimental groups start behind the conventional ones, there should be better results with the kinds of financial support they receive. Finally, we rarely hear what happens when support ends or studies are completed. Do the effects of the reform continue or do they stop? Was this a long-term solution or only a stopgap one? Who bears the costs of sustaining its activities? Were the study conclusions implemented? The cases that follow will look at some of these issues in more detail.

CHAPTER 3

THE EGYPT CASE: USAID SUPPORT FOR PRIMARY EDUCATION (1979–1990)

BACKGROUND[1]

Modern public education for boys was established in Egypt starting in the nineteenth century primarily as a means of creating a civil service for the British colonial administration. Most students in government schools came from less affluent classes. Elites hired European governesses and tutors to teach their children at home including, in some cases, girls. Boys were taught in the "practical" English of politics and business, while girls learned in "more cultivated" French. The first girls' school in Egypt was established in 1829 by the foreign Church Missionary Society and the first government girls' school in 1873 under the Khedive's wife. These initiatives, however, only provided education to a limited number of students.

Compulsory education became law in Egypt's first constitution of 1923, and was reiterated as a goal after Independence in 1952 when the new government declared its intention to provide education for all citizens. However it lacked the means to provide sufficient opportunities, and as the numbers of enrolling children increased the limited facilities soon became overcrowded and the quality of the academic program declined. Education became popular quickly because it was the main route for a poor rural or urban child to move up the social ladder into the middle classes.[2] Graduates of universities automatically qualified for civil service jobs offered by the government. Soon conservative parents who had not valued modern schooling began sending boys to government schools "to increase their employment opportunities," and later sent girls "to make them better wives and mothers." Ultimately, most Egyptians accepted the idea of coeducation in some grades[3] and technical, civil service, and professional jobs for women.

Along with Lebanon and Syria, Egypt was one of the leaders in modern education in the Arab World, and one of the first to introduce secular education.[4] When countries like Saudi Arabia and Yemen opened their own education systems from the 1960s on, they hired staff from Egypt, Syria, and the Sudan where an oversupply of trained government teachers made these jobs attractive.[5]

Still, girls in these early years remained underrepresented in Egypt's education system. Even though their actual numbers rose significantly along with those of boys, their ratios of primary enrollments stagnated at only about 38 percent of total enrollments in the 40 years between 1930 and 1970. A major reason was a lack of infrastructure that capped the supply of schooling places, despite valiant efforts of school staff to expand opportunities by increasing class size, establishing two or three school shifts a day, and using other creative means.[6]

A revised constitution in 1971 again reiterated the principle of free education for Egyptian citizens, but this time extended it through the university level. Law 139 of 1981 made education compulsory to the end of the preparatory level (ninth grade) but again because of a scarcity of spaces the law was impossible to enforce. Other rules set age limits on participation. Children could not enter primary school after their eighth birthday and in practice could not enter school if they had no birth certificate; they had to leave primary school if they had not graduated by age fourteen. As a result many children found their participation limited, especially in rural areas where many had no record of their births.[7]

CONDITIONS IN THE LATE 1970S WHEN USAID BEGAN ITS SUPPORT

By the late 1970s and early 1980s when USAID was starting to support Egyptian education, the country's population stood at around 70 million, with a high birth rate that added a million children every 9 months. Of these millions, 95 percent lived in the 10 percent of fertile land bordering the Nile. The rest were either nomadic or living in scattered oases that were difficult to reach with education services. Rural populations at the time exceeded urban populations, but by the end of the twentieth century the majority of the population lived in urban areas.

The Egyptian population is culturally homogeneous, with the major differences among groups being those of social class and religious affiliation. The majority of Egyptians are Sunni Muslims but there is a roughly 10–20 percent minority group of Christians (Copt, Catholic, Greek and Roman Orthodox, Protestant, and Anglican). The gap between rich and poor is significant and continues to grow. Arabic is the official language but most educated Egyptians speak English. Fluency in English has major social, professional, and economic advantages, and usually only those who attend private schools can achieve high enough levels of English to qualify for more lucrative private-sector jobs.

By the end of the 1970s, the largest group of out-of-school children was girls, particularly in rural areas. Only about half (54 percent) of girls of primary age were enrolled (versus 70 percent of children overall).[8] Despite the fact that girls' enrollments were increasing at one and a half times the rate of boys, most of the gains occurred in urban areas and a significant gender gap remained. By 1981, 85 percent of females were still illiterate.[9] Literacy figures however mainly reflect earlier decades before schooling opportunities were as available for girls, and consequently they are less effective as measures of recent efforts to enroll girls.

Education in Egypt was and still is delivered through three systems: a formal government system, a large private system, and a religious system[10] with two levels—the Al Azhar College of primary through secondary grades, and Al Azhar University. The government's definition of basic education in the 1970s consisted of six years of primary and three years of preparatory. Children advanced automatically at grades one and three and through succeeding on local exams at grades two, four and five. As an incentive to keep children in school national testing didn't occur until grades eight or nine.

The federal Ministry of Education (MOE) assumes responsibility for education planning, policy formation, technical supervision, quality control, coordination among the branches, and setting rules and regulations. In the 1970s Egypt was divided into 26 administrative units or governorates that were further subdivided into districts. The governorates were responsible for the direct operation of schools and implementing national policy according to directives from the federal ministry. Overall the formal system was highly centralized with little independent decision making at the regional level. As a result local management was weak, with staff referring essentially all administrative details back to the MOE. Program quality could not be reformed at the local level since instructional policy and inputs came from central authorities who knew little of what went on in classrooms.

PROBLEMS REQUIRING DONOR ASSISTANCE

In the late 1970s it was obvious to everyone that there were fundamental problems with education in Egypt. Most obvious were overcrowded classrooms, deteriorating infrastructure, and inadequate capacity to meet the massive demand for schooling by the Egyptian people. Poor pay caused teachers to neglect teaching in the classrooms and focus on after school "private lessons" where they could increase their income severalfold. Many parents found it difficult to support the costs of "free education" that included paying for uniforms, incidentals, private lessons, and the lost opportunity costs of forgoing their children's work. Program quality—defined by pass rates on exams that primarily tested memorized facts—was deteriorating as class size increased and less qualified teachers were recruited to cope with the increased number of children. Education officials were stifled by a lethargic bureaucracy and limited budgets. Even if they had wanted to plan more effectively there were few reliable tools with which to work—data collection was rudimentary and analyses limited to tallies of data for administrative purposes. Civil service rules with automatic seniority offered little incentive for staff to make changes, and there were few ways to hold teachers and officials accountable for results. In short the education system followed the forms of education—rules for building codes and hiring staff, exams, and teaching—but functioned poorly, and few bureaucrats felt anything could be done to improve matters.

Despite the general acknowledgment that there were serious problems, federal officials[11] knew surprisingly little about how schools worked, how training was conducted, how textbooks were produced, or how local exams were developed.

The Context of Schooling

Sources of Resistance to Schooling

In the 1970s Egyptian officials claimed that low enrollments, especially of girls, were due to the conservative beliefs of rural parents who saw little need for education. Coupled with these views, they said, were poverty and the importance of child labor in agriculture and household work. But those who studied the problem suggested that low enrollments were at least as much due to the lack of accessible facilities. Local officials facing overcrowded classes often refused admission to girls when there were insufficient places for boys, and academically weak children of both sexes were encouraged to drop out by overworked teachers trying to reduce the numbers in their classes.

Historic Lag in Girls' Enrollments

One study[12] showed girls' enrollments at all levels lagging behind those of boys historically, especially in rural areas, until in modern times they became almost equal. Extended education was first perceived as a means of expanding work opportunities and increasing the social status of the lower classes. It was therefore viewed as of greater benefit to boys and, by extension, their families. Girls would eventually be supported by their husbands and take on their status. However, once a critical mass of boys enrolled, parents began enrolling a few daughters to "make them better partners and mothers."[13] Over time—and this varied from a few years to more than a decade depending on the area—more girls enrolled until it became a norm for most boys and girls to attend. The same lag occurred at each level of schooling. Many early enrollers of both sexes also dropped out early, but soon more children persisted to the end of primary and then to the end of university where they qualified for guaranteed government jobs. Unless a child planned to go through the stages to the end of university there was little benefit in struggling with difficult primary completion exams. As a consequence many children dropped out just before these exams. Literacy only had limited usefulness in villages, but university degrees could lead to a better life, beyond anything a villager could achieve in farming.

As the costs of "free education" mounted and children moved to cities for jobs, parents began to look more carefully at the talents of their children. They might support lengthy education for academically inclined sons and daughters and technical/vocational training or apprenticeships for manually inclined sons. Where education "didn't take," rural parents kept a son and daughter barely literate to ensure they had help with farming and household work. For girls, the first impulse toward education was to enhance their desirability as marriage partners. Eventually however academically gifted girls also persisted long enough to claim government jobs.[14] As professionals bringing respect and dignity to their families, they were accepted into the work force in a way poor women working as servants or manual laborers were not. The latter cast a shadow on their men folk who by implication could not be fulfilling their traditional support roles if their women had to work. Girls who dropped out early usually married quickly[15] or stayed home to help their parents.

While educators felt all children should enroll and finish compulsory education, these family decisions about sending or limiting children's participation were much more rational than they might otherwise seem in terms of a rural family's needs at the time. The decisions allowed families to diversify their future options in a country where most of the older people could not look forward to social security or pension benefits.[16] Investment in schooling for boys, from a rural parent's perspective, could become a safety net to ensure family income even when the sons moved to distant cities and had families of their own.

But again although general reasons for resistance to education were known, the details were disputed. If government officials were right, the fault lay with ignorant parents, and if parents were right they lay with the government for not providing sufficient facilities, making education too costly, and providing poor quality programs where children found it difficult to succeed. Schooling often didn't seem relevant or worthwhile to the rural families most resistant to sending children to school.

Reluctance to Assist the Education Sector

Up until the 1970s USAID had been reluctant to support large-scale education projects in the region. The reasoning was that education sectors in most developing countries would require vast sums of funding to make an impact on their huge school systems. And the solutions would be complex, requiring large administrative staffs to oversee any prospective projects. It was also unclear where USAID would find adequate counterparts when poorly educated bureaucrats and insufficient budgets seemed largely responsible for governments like Egypt's being unable to manage their education sectors. The donors were also unimpressed with local nongovernmental organizations (NGOs), seeing them as focusing too narrowly on specific groups of beneficiaries, using suspect accounting practices, and with only limited management skills. The assessment was mostly correct in Egypt at the time where the vast majority of NGOs were inspired by religious and charitable motives. Many were staffed by upper-class volunteers or poorly paid personnel who lacked the management skills that might make them reliable partners in any large-scale education project.

Why Egypt?

Why was there a sudden interest in supporting a large education project in Egypt? For a long time policy makers realized that education or lack thereof was affecting every important social indictor in developing countries—health, fertility, economic opportunities, and women's status, and unless children were better educated, the future was likely to bring more of the same. For Egypt a convenient opportunity arose in the Camp David Peace Accords that were concluded in 1978. In exchange for signing final peace agreements, Egypt and Israel were both promised significant financial support by the US Government to help in the development of their countries.[17] Egypt's funds were to be roughly comparable to the nonmilitary subsidies given to the Israelis. The difference was that while the United States gave checks to the Israelis to spend as they wanted, they insisted upon overseeing Egyptian assistance to ensure that resources would benefit the Egyptian people. The funds were considerable, causing the dilemma for USAID of how their limited staff in Cairo could oversee the number of projects that would be needed to consume so much money. Suddenly in Egypt the high costs of working in the education sector no longer seemed so prohibitive.

USAID SUPPORT FOR BASIC EDUCATION IN EGYPT (1979–1990)

Project Activities

The case that follows describes three of the main activities USAID supported in basic education between 1979 and 1990:[18]

- A survey of basic education in Egypt (1979) to assess the need for support;
- The Basic Education[19] Development Project (BEDP) (1980 to 1990); and
- Studies of USAID contributions to basic education in Egypt (1982 to 1985).

The case describes the roles of assistance personnel in identifying needs, in carrying out reforms, and in evaluating the impact of interventions.

Activity One: A Survey of Basic Education in Egypt (1979)

The Goals and the Data Collection

From discussions in the MOE it became clear that officials knew little about how the education sector worked in the countryside. Officials knew the rules and regulations that directed administrators in their work but were not aware of how these principles were actually put into practice in schools and classrooms.

To find out more about the way the sector worked, USAID contracted a team, through a US-based consulting company, to conduct a comprehensive study of the basic education system in Egypt. The joint Egyptian-US Educational Survey Team consisted of twenty-four Egyptian members selected by the MOE and ten American consultants. The team was charged by the MOE with identifying reforms in three areas: reforms that would increase the enrollments of children to 90 percent of the six- to twelve-year old cohort by 1990, adapt the academic program to address the need for a better-prepared work force, and finally to develop responsible citizens of Egypt. A major goal was to reduce the disparities in opportunities by region, class, geography, and sex. The MOE also wanted an expansion of preparatory and secondary education, teachers' training, and technical and higher education to accommodate the larger numbers of children that would be completing primary level if the project succeeded.

The team spent three months[20] in the field looking into all aspects of the education system—visiting schools and training institutions in various parts of Egypt and learning about the administrative structures at all levels of the bureaucracy, from the central ministry to the governorates, districts, and schools.

Findings

The "Report of the Joint Egyptian-US Survey Team on Basic Education in Egypt" summarized the team's findings based on their discussions with Egyptians at all levels of the education system. It described the major strengths and weaknesses of the existing system and recommended options for external assistance. Based on ministry data the team found that about three million children remained out of school and their numbers were growing rapidly. The existing system only provided opportunities for roughly four million primary students (about 68 percent of the total children ages six to twelve) and 1.5 million preparatory students. That meant capacity would have to double just to absorb these children and keep up with population growth.

According to the report, the main strengths of the existing system were:

- MOE officials expressed strong support for expanding education to all children.
- There was MOE consensus on the need for reform and the areas where improvements should be made (exams, buildings, curriculum, and training).

- The public showed enthusiasm for schooling and as a result the rates of enrolled children (68 percent of six- to twelve-year olds and 78 percent of six-year olds) were rising rapidly, especially among girls and rural children.
- There was growing consensus that education needed to become more practical, and that technical secondary options should also increase.

There was also capacity in the Egyptian system to expand within existing supervisory/administrative systems, training institutions, and publishing venues. Research capacity also existed in universities and semigovernmental bodies to conduct evaluations and studies.[21] And finally several "model school" experiments had been tried in Egypt that might provide a template for change.[22]

The report also described the major obstacles to reform:

- The remaining large disparities in access to education opportunities;
- Inadequate physical infrastructure in both quality and quantity;
- Poor teacher training and issues of teacher supply especially in rural areas;
- Shortages of instructional materials and equipment;
- An academic bias that was likely to discourage practical courses;
- A lack of capacity to plan and set priorities;
- Weaknesses in collection and analysis of education data;
- Overly centralized decision making; and
- Weaknesses in financial management data and systems.

The main recommendations[23] of the team were to

- prepare a school building design to meet local needs and that would use local materials and involve local participation;[24]
- develop pilot "basic education" instructional models that stress teacher effectiveness and utilization;

- strengthen research and curriculum development capacities by establishing special units in Cairo and in the governorates;
- strengthen instructional materials development, production, and distribution;
- strengthen financial management, planning, and budgeting;
- develop and test more effective educational assessment/ measurement systems, procedures, and instruments;
- expand planning, management training, and reorganization of the central MOE as part of a full decentralization effort;
- expand and diversify technical education options after the basic education stage, including training for teachers of practical courses in basic education; and
- coordinate basic education with opportunities for nonformal skills training and adult education.

This long list of mostly vaguely stated recommendations, if implemented, would have shaped the way all departments of the MOE operated. In effect by assembling a team whose specialties encompassed all these areas, it was inevitable that the recommendations would extend across this broad range of recommendations. In retrospect a failure of the survey was in listing recommendations separately, without prioritizing them or showing how they were interconnected. As a result project designers were free to pick and choose activities without fully recognizing how they influenced one another.

After condensing the general and specific recommendations of the report, the overall issues became (1) the critical lack of facilities for schooling and the shortage of female teachers to teach in rural schools; (2) the poor quality of the academic program, where the lack of quality inputs, the emphasis on rote learning, an exam system designed to weed out children rather than measure their skills, and harsh discipline tended to discourage enrollments, persistence, and learning. And finally (3) an overly centralized bureaucracy unable to plan or manage well because it lacked the tools and know-how, and because even the most insignificant decisions were made at the center far from the source of most problems.

Activity Two: Implementation of BEDP

Although the team had recommended a comprehensive set of reforms for Egypt's education system, USAID settled on four main ones:

- Building primary schools and classrooms, and modestly increasing downstream preparatory facilities for the larger numbers of primary graduates;
- Making education more relevant for primary students by mounting practical courses and providing needed equipment and supplies;
- Working on policy reforms to increase the number of trained rural teachers; and
- Building an effective Educational Management Information System (EMIS).

This case examines three of the components: school construction, practical courses, and the efforts to increase the number of rural women teachers. An EMIS was developed over this period, but while school data became more reliable the MOE staff was only beginning to use it more effectively by the time the main BEP project ended.

Building Schools, Classrooms, and Facilities to Increase Student Enrollments

The main intervention of BEDP and its most costly was the construction of schools. Over ten years (1981 to 1991), USAID committed $190 million to school construction. The aim according to project documents was to increase the enrollments of rural children, especially girls, between the ages of six and fifteen in grades one through nine. The schools were built mainly in rural areas where girls' enrollments were low, no schools were available, or schools were incomplete or severely crowded. USAID set a target of 1,300 schools, funded a design for the schools, and in preparation for construction conducted a school mapping survey.

The USAID school design came in multiples of six classrooms. On the basis of the size of their estimated school-going populations, most villages received either six- or twelve-classroom models.[25] The buildings were painted a distinctive color to make them recognizable as USAID-funded schools. In most cases communities provided the land, often communal land like a reaping floor or land that was not useful for agriculture because it was too swampy or rocky. Most of the schools were built in rural villages, but some were constructed on the outskirts of large towns where the pressures for schooling were escalating.

USAID and the MOE agreed that after completion of the new schools, they would be turned over to the MOE for repair and maintenance. However several years after construction many of the schools were in disrepair, badly in need of painting, with leaking or no longer functioning latrine and water facilities, broken windows, and unusable school grounds because of trash build-up or standing water.[26] Many of the schools also became overcrowded,[27] and soon were hardly distinguishable from the poorly maintained government schools except for their distinctive colors.

The new schools absorbed the largest part of BEDP funding. Schools were costly in themselves, but became more so when contractors bid low to get the contracts and then cut expenses with slipshod construction and poor quality materials. Some observers estimated that because of corrupt contractors it cost up to 30 percent more per building because of the redundancy that had to be built into the structures to make them safe. To manage construction USAID hired an Egyptian engineer to work with MOE officials to choose appropriate locations for the schools and oversee the local engineering firms who supervised the work. Payment to contractors was geared to prearranged milestones in the construction process.

Construction Results

By the end of the ten-year project 1,949 (rather than the anticipated 1,300) schools were built and a USAID document noted a rise in female primary participation from 36 to 42 percent of total enrollments in rural areas of Egypt. In urban areas girls' enrollments rose 26 percent over the period while boys' enrollments rose 16 percent.[28] According to an evaluation report the schools brought in 900,000 children each year, with 360,000 of them girls. By 1990 data showed that 90 percent of eligible Egyptian children were enrolled in school, up 10 percent from the start of the project in 1980.[29] There could be no doubt that USAID's roughly 2,000 schools along with the few schools the Egyptian Government built over that period contributed importantly to increasing enrollment.[30] Since few schools had been built during the 1960s and 1970s, there had been a strong need for these buildings.

In the final evaluations, the USAID supervisor in charge of overseeing school construction was commended for the impressive job he had done to ensure the solid construction of the schools and for completing more than the planned total. While 2,000 schools were a significant start in meeting the demand for education in Egypt, they only comprised 13 percent of the primary schools and school sections in Egypt. During the decade of construction, the USAID schools increased enrollments above already established trends of rising enrollments, but they were not responsible for all new enrollments as claimed. Contributing to the increases was the escalating use of shifts by Egyptian authorities to crowd more children into existing schools.[31]

Even though most of the schools constructed by USAID were primary schools, enrollments also increased at the preparatory level from the pressures of primary school graduates. Female enrollments at the preparatory level rose in rural areas from less than 30 percent (180,000) to 40 percent (700,000) of total enrollments, and, in the four governorates of Upper Egypt where girls' enrollments had been lowest before the project their rates grew at even faster rates. Meanwhile in urban areas where USAID had not built any schools, girls' participation rates doubled, reinforcing the idea that adding shifts and more children per class accounted for many of the increases.

As far as USAID was concerned the construction component not only proved successful at increasing participation but it helped alleviate the problem of expending the vast sums provided under the Camp David agreements without unreasonably taxing its own staff. It was a win-win situation for everyone, even though there remained considerable need for more schooling spaces.

Teacher-Related Reforms to Increase Enrollments

USAID was concerned that in building rural schools there might not be enough teachers to staff them, especially female staff members who were needed to encourage the participation of girls. When urban teachers were assigned to rural schools they either had to find lodging in the village or commute long distances. Both options were costly and women found it difficult if they had children and household obligations. The solution, authorities believed, was to find and train educated men and women from villages where schools were located. But entry into training institutes was based largely on scores from secondary school exams[32] where rural students tended to do less well. USAID persuaded the MOE to admit rural students, especially women, to fill the gap. At the time educators genuinely believed teacher training was the essential ingredient to producing quality programs, even though no studies had been conducted to determine whether training produced better teaching or improved student learning. Over the course of BEDP the number of qualified rural teachers increased, and undoubtedly reduced teacher absenteeism. It may also have made local teachers feel more accountable for student learning and less harsh in disciplining children, given their need to maintain good relations with their neighbors.

Deteriorating Program Quality

By expanding the pool of teacher candidates however to less academically qualified individuals, the policy may also have contributed to the decreasing quality of the academic program. An Egyptian researcher Nader Fergany and his colleagues reported that "indicators of primary education, which had made good progress up to the mid 1980s, had begun to decline" and by the late 1980s, as BEDP was completing its initial phase, were definitely in decline. The indicators he is talking about are "the proportion of entrants who completed the primary cycle, the average speed of completing the cycle, the proportion of primary completers in the population at large, and school quality as measured by test scores which had never been very high."[33] A study of data from the same period by Hanushek and Lavy found that poor school quality was also having a significant impact on enrollment and participation.[34] What seems to be clear from these studies is that during the 1980s while BEDP was being implemented, school quality was declining and may also have had a negative impact on the participation of some children.

Despite BEDP, the pressures to increase schooling opportunities continued and in 1989/90 near the end of the project the minister of education decided to open more places in schools by abolishing the sixth grade and making the basic education cycle eight rather than nine years. This meant one or more extra classrooms would become available in every primary school. This change however caused an unwieldy double cohort to wend its way through the system up through university with issues at every level about teachers, exams, and admissions to the next stage. After several years of deteriorating exam scores, the sixth grade was reinstated—with new issues of space and teachers to accommodate the newly introduced extra year of schooling.

Mounting Practical Courses

Following the UN definition of basic education as comprising a more relevant curriculum that included prevocational skills, BEDP supported "practical courses" for Egyptian schools that taught these skills. These were supposed to be skills that children could use in their homes or, with continued training, turn into a vocation.[35] BEDP delivered

20 million dollars worth of equipment for grades five through nine in 15,000 schools and supported the training of 13,500 basic education teachers. The Egyptians agreed to provide raw materials once the initial supply ran out.

The BEDP equipment kits included ones for carpentry, electricity, maritime activities, agriculture, and home economics. A school was to receive a particular kit based on the local economy; for example, a school on the northern coast might receive maritime equipment while a school in a farming community would receive the agriculture kit. In most schools girls took the home economics course that received a stove and utensils. Educators felt the courses would make education more appealing to children who could use the new skills to improve their homes and communities.

Activity Three: BEDP's Study of USAID Contributions to Basic Education

Study Questions

There were still many questions relating to education in Egypt and the potential of USAID's assistance activities. Would the new schools actually attract new students or simply make existing schools less crowded? What were the reasons behind the resistance to schooling in rural areas? Would parents change their views about enrolling girls if a school were accessible nearby? How would practical courses be viewed and would they have the intended impact? Would children persist longer in school? These were some of the questions USAID wanted answered in its first major support for education in the region.

Study Design

To answer some of these questions, USAID funded an intensive study of BEDP contributions to basic education. The study had three aims:

- To separate the "real" impact of new school construction on children's participation from the effects of general trends;

- To identify factors affecting family decisions about children's participation; and
- To determine the effectiveness of practical courses.

The study compared ten USAID school sites with a matched group of non-USAID sites. A site consisted of a cluster of schools in a catchment area that drew on the same population of students. The sites were divided into "very rural" and "less rural" based on their proximity to population centers, and were located in a variety of Egyptian contexts in Upper and Lower Egypt. Research teams visited the sites twice a year to collect data, interview parents, and observe the teaching of practical courses. The timing of the visits to new school sites occurred if possible before school construction began and in all cases after schools opened. The control sites were visited at the same times—twice a year over a three-year period.

The Impact of School Construction on Children's Participation

The researchers first identified historic trends in school-level data for all the cluster sites, and then determined whether the trajectory in enrollments changed after the new school opened. The study then looked at enrollments in the new school clusters and compared them with the control clusters where there was no new school. It was hypothesized that once new schools were built closer to their homes, some children might withdraw from the old school and enroll in the new one with no effect on the total children enrolling in the catchment area as a whole. This however did not turn out to be true. More children enrolled in the catchment area than would have been predicted by ongoing trends, probably because of the role distance plays in the school-going behavior of rural children, especially girls. The study drew the following conclusions about the USAID clusters:

- The first year after USAID schools opened, grade one enrollments increased an average of 41 students or 18 percent per school cluster over the clusters without a USAID school.

- The second year 30 grade one students were added over the trend expectation—fewer than the first year because of a smaller pool of eligible students.
- In years three and four, the numbers added declined to 29 and 22, and after that the increases reflected population growth rates.
- In the first year each USAID cluster site retained 87 students (9 percent) in grades two through six above the trend expectation. In the next three years 127 (12 percent), 104 (9 percent), and 122 (11 percent) were retained above the expectation.
- In the first year after construction, increases were also higher among the target "more rural" students (23 percent) compared with "less rural" students (16 percent), and among girls (23 percent) compared with boys (16 percent). In subsequent years the figures for girls and boys were 19 and 8 percent, 15 and 8 percent, and 9 and 7 percent, respectively. Girls and economically disadvantaged groups also persisted longer at these clusters than at non-USAID cluster sites.
- At the rates of repetition and dropout in USAID sites, seven out of ten children would complete primary in the expected six-year period, two would drop out and one would repeat one or more grades. If an effort was made to halve this wastage rate in the country as a whole it would be equivalent to increasing school space by the equivalent of 428 schools at the then current school size.[36]
- The average reduction in crowding per site was 99 students or 44 percent of the population of the average new school. This condition was created when students left their old schools to enter new schools leaving behind either more spaces for new students or a less crowded situation.

Study figures in sum confirmed that new USAID-funded schools had a definite impact on participation rates and specifically on targeted groups within the areas where they were built. Moreover MOE figures showed that in the final five years of the 1980s the fastest growth rates for enrollment occurred among rural primary (30 percent) and preparatory (25 percent) girls than had ever been seen before.

Factors Affecting Family Decisions about School Going

Study data showed in more detail the factors that go into family decisions about whether or not to send children to school. Remember, school officials at the start of the project blamed parents for not enrolling their children and not keeping them in school. The intensive study of families interviewed hundreds of family members to identify the factors affecting children's participation.[37] The household survey showed the following:

- The major factors influencing parents' decisions about schooling were distance,[38] school crowding, poverty, costs, lack of relevance, and need for child labor.
- When parents were asked why they didn't send their children to school, many claimed the reason was poverty. However, researchers felt parents might be stressing this factor since it made their decision seem beyond their control (poverty clearly did not prevent other families from sending their children). When asked why other parents didn't send children, the majority blamed it on their "neglect" or "ignorance."
- Other reasons included the need to accompany girls to school (and having no appropriate person available), special obstacles like major roads or rivers that posed problems for young children, family feuds that endangered children on the way to school, the inconvenience of a school shift's timing that interfered with a child's work, et cetera.
- Some parents said they preferred the Al-Azhar religious schools rather than the secular system because Al-Azhar schools were truly free and led more easily to university entry (requiring only high school passing exams).
- The main factors affecting dropout were usually school-related: failed exams, physical punishment, repetition, and gender-related issues of teasing or inadequate bathroom facilities that made schools unpleasant for girls. Once again

economic factors such as poverty, schooling costs, and the need for child labor were cited as reasons for dropout.
- Parents said they preferred to send boys to the older established schools farther away from their homes that they believed provided a better education, but enrolled their daughters in the closer new schools.
- One important finding was that girls' enrollments dropped off significantly if schools were more than 1.5 kilometers away from their homes.
- An unexpected finding was that many rural parents who had expressed strong reservations about girls' education before a new school was built changed their minds and sent the girls once a school was constructed nearby.
- Parents universally said that they sent boys to school for better economic opportunities, and girls to make them better wives and mothers ("it illuminates their lives").[39]

These studies of family attitudes confirm much of what was known already about school-going, along with a few new details that shed light on rural parental decision making. But they also suggest caution in using any one source of opinion data or any moment in time as the most authentic. Teachers and parents expressed radically different views about the reasons for children enrolling or not enrolling mainly based, it seemed, on wanting to deflect blame from themselves. Teachers said the problem was "ignorant" rural parents, while parents blamed the school staff for making schooling unpleasant. Similarly parents changed their opinions about girls' education almost immediately when they saw their neighbors sending their daughters to new nearby schools.

The Effectiveness of the Practical Courses

A team of researchers also conducted classroom observations to assess the effectiveness of the USAID-funded practical courses. This component was plagued with difficulties from the start. The equipment often didn't make sense: a "lawn edger" for agriculture, for example, or an electric stove where schools didn't have electricity and families cooked on small kerosene burners. Teachers, even though "trained" in their use, reverted to rote methods, saying for example: "This is a hammer. What is it children?" "A hammer." "The hammer is used to hit nails. What is it used for?" "To hit nails." Teachers who actually taught children to use a hammer soon ran out of wood and had to buy more from their own pockets or revert to demonstrations to conserve materials. The products, such as tissue boxes, were not of much use in rural homes in any case.

Meanwhile parents complained that the courses took time from the academic studies; children needed to pass exams (practical courses didn't count for grades and therefore were not regarded as important). Parents felt "regional" skills like agriculture could be better taught at home than in school.[40] "If you want to help children get jobs," they said, "teach them accounting and clerical skills so they can work in offices" "We send them to school to escape agriculture."

Lessons from Egypt

While there is no doubt that BEDP accomplished its main aim of increasing opportunities for rural children to enter and stay in school, it is still possible to learn other important lessons from the project.

The Consequence of Focusing Exclusively on Quantity

With its attention and resources focused mainly on construction, USAID gave little attention to improving the academic program. To be fair, at the time, there was little idea of what "quality" involved, and curriculum reform was considered too sensitive for foreign involvement. Also, a commonly held view was that quality could be achieved simply by training teachers to do a better job. Little weight was given to whether new teaching approaches fit the schooling context, books, or exams or whether training that worked abroad would work in the local environment. In any case, USAID probably would have been reluctant to oversee a project as complicated as one encompassing the variety of inputs that might be needed to improve the academic program.

As was true for other development agencies at the time, USAID was intent on getting children, and especially girls, into school. Educators often noted that actions to encourage girls' participation would also encourage boys' participation, while others believed that if only one generation of girls went to school the problem of educating future generations would be solved since they would send their children.[41] They believed poor academic programs were better than none, and if children only persisted long enough most would learn to read and write. These views overlooked some important factors—that many children didn't remain long enough in school to achieve functional literacy, that those who failed exams and repeated grades were occupying places that could have been filled by others, and that the inefficiencies of dropouts and repeaters were raising per-graduate costs of schooling to very high levels. Even those students who absorbed the maximum from schooling were not fully prepared with the critical thinking and other skills they and Egypt needed to develop their full capacities. Any Egyptian family that could afford to do so was sending its children to private schools where it was believed they would acquire better skills.

The Interconnectedness of the System

Perhaps the most important lesson from Egypt is that education delivery exists in a complex system where every part affects every other part. Changes in one create changes in others that are not always desirable. Quantity and quality are so inextricably intertwined that they are not easily disengaged.[42] By concentrating on schooling spaces USAID inadvertently weakened the academic program when less-qualified teaching staff were brought in to handle the increases. Similarly when "relevant" practical courses were added to the schedule, less time was available for academic studies, further contributing to the decline in exam scores as Fergany's studies show.

Other Lessons

Other general lessons from this early support for Egyptian education included the following:

- The important part politics played in project considerations, in this case by determining funding levels, what to fund, and how to implement reforms. Local politics played a role in locating schools, deciding technical specifications for buildings, and in awarding construction contracts.
- Even thorough needs assessment surveys were unable to guarantee a trouble-free project or predict all outcomes such as the failure of practical courses or the rapidity with which parental attitudes would change. This suggests the importance of keeping designs flexible so they can adjust to the inevitable problems and opportunities that arise.
- Project implementers should have become aware much sooner of the negative consequences of large student increases on the quality of programs. The studies that were monitoring impacts (essentially formative[43] evaluations) should possibly have noted and suggested midcourse corrections earlier but they did not, nor did they feel this was within their narrow mandate of focusing on whether USAID contributions worked.
- Bureaucratic rigidities of both donors and recipients limited reforms. While strict local rules and procedures helped avoid favoritism and haphazard implementation, they made construction substantially more costly and didn't address the important issue of corrupt contractors. The critical issue of "private lessons" was also never addressed even though it played and still plays a significant role in suppressing participation and in discouraging effective instruction in classrooms.
- Studies were an important way for policy makers to understand how rural families make education decisions and potentially how they might address these issues.
- The studies showed that the opinions of different groups of stakeholders can vary widely. Entirely different activities might have been designed from listening to only one

side—parents or school personnel. This underscores the importance of listening to all those with a stake in reform, while remaining aware that opinions can change quickly once new conditions exist.

- A novel program like the "practical courses" should have been piloted in a limited area before taking it to scale. This might have averted a costly failure. Parents and teachers were only asked about it after the fact.
- Parents' decisions about educating their children turned out to be more rational than first expected. If educators believe all children need an education, they need to address the main reasons parents keep them home.[44] This project brought schools closer to some children's homes but it did not address other reasons children remained out of school such as need for their labor or the incidental costs of schooling.

As the first major USAID-supported education project in the region, it was not surprising to find among the successes that there were also weaknesses and unexpected failures. The preproject activities in certain ways were exemplary: a team of well-experienced American experts paired with Egyptian educators and a leisurely three months to survey all aspects of the Egyptian system. The team's reports were comprehensive and far-reaching thanks to the nuanced understandings provided by Egyptian team members.[45] USAID quite reasonably limited the scope of interventions to ones that could be managed by its staff after contracting much of the work out to Egyptian and American companies. In addition to the construction activities, practical courses, policy changes, and the studies described above, there were also improvements in the way data was gathered and analyzed (EMIS). But in the end the project left major gaps unfilled and it is knowledge of these critical gaps and weaknesses that undoubtedly led USAID to modify its assistance to countries like Pakistan.

After BEDP

US assistance did not stop with BEDP in Egypt. In 1997 USAID reviewed its efforts worldwide to reduce sex disparities in access, participation, and retention. The review[46] concluded that disparities persisted because donor-funded reforms focused so heavily on girls' participation without improving the education program generally. Many programs addressing gender equity had been underfunded, and relegated to remote parts of the bureaucracy. The authors concluded that education reform would fail if it didn't also address the community barriers that prevented girls and women from reaping the benefits of education.

As a result of the review, USAID changed its strategy to strengthening education systems in general and in particular focusing on the needs of girls and women. The Agency concluded

- Focusing on the quality aspects of girls' education would also strengthen the quality of primary education for boys.[47]
- Promoting girls' education required a multisectoral approach involving communities, public and private sectors, the media, and civil society.
- Using USAID funds and activities to catalyze local resources for girls' education could have a multiplier effect that would encourage buy-in from other agencies and coordination of their efforts.

For the next several years USAID designed programs to carry out these principles: the Girls' and Women's Education Activity (GWEA) in several countries stressed community participation in education projects and multisectoral approaches to coordinate local resources.[48] As noted in the previous chapter GWEA had a number of important successes, but there were also drawbacks. With finite resources, money has to be invested judiciously. When the choice required mobilizing communities to support schools,[49] it meant fewer resources available to reform the school program system itself. As we have seen in the Egypt case, it can be the poor quality of school programs that dampens the interest in participation. The multisectoral approach was able to raise funds and volunteer support from outside the school system, but not without considerable expenditure to mobilize that support.[50]

The Pakistan project that started less than a decade later showed that USAID learned much from its experiences in Egypt. Among other lessons, USAID approached the Pakistani system more comprehensively by addressing both quality and quantity issues, and by encouraging local officials to take their own initiatives in reforming local institutions.

Chapter 4

The Pakistan Case: USAID Support for Primary Education (1987–1994)

Background[1]

For Muslims, education has a long history in the subcontinent going back to the advent of Islam and the rich culture Arab traders brought to the region. Between the thirteenth and eighteenth centuries the main centers of learning for Muslims were small schools adjacent to mosques where children memorized the Koran and learned the everyday practices of Islam. Some adolescents continued their studies with Islamic scholars who taught them the meanings, jurisprudence, and theological implications of the Koran and the *Hadith* (the sayings and examples of the Prophet Muhammad).

Eventually small Koranic schools proliferated across the region in villages populated by Muslims until there were few settlements that didn't have a *madrasa*. For the most part the learning was rote and children were expected to accept the written documents and their teachers' pronouncements uncritically. The aim of this education was to transmit the original meanings accurately, relying on sources as close to the time of the Prophet as possible. An important point was that children in much of the region were memorizing the texts in Arabic, a language that was not a mother tongue in the subcontinent and consequently their understanding of the content was limited until they were older and able to listen to the interpretations of their teachers. Eventually when "modern" education was introduced, this pattern of rote teaching/learning was transferred to the study of secular subjects where textbooks and teachers simply took the place of the authoritative religious documents and scholars.

This *madrasa* system continued to form the basis of education for many Muslims even after the British took over (in 1757) and in 1835 established a modern system with English as the medium of instruction. By 1854 there was a rapid spread of Western education across the subcontinent including three universities in the main cities of Calcutta, Bombay, and Madras by 1857. Most of the students at these universities were Hindus, with few Muslims studying at that level until a university was especially opened for them in 1875. During that time the remote northwestern portions of India that later became Pakistan received few education services, and continued to rely on the *madrasa* system to educate children.

Before the partition of Pakistan from India, few Muslims entered Western schools and for the most part shunned government service. One reason was that the British had blamed the Muslims for the Mutiny of 1857 and thereafter the Muslims had withdrawn into their own communities. Only after the Aligarh movement was formed by members of the Muslim community were they brought back into the mainstream.

British rule ended on the subcontinent in 1947 and as demanded by the Muslim League, India was partitioned to provide a separate homeland for the Muslims. A majority of India's Muslim population moved to the new nation of Pakistan, although about a third remained in India. Pakistan at the time was divided into East and West Pakistan, until in 1971 East Pakistan broke off and became Bangladesh.

Conditions in the Late 1980s When USAID Began Its Support

Pakistan was left with some of the least developed areas of the Indian subcontinent especially in the remote provinces of the Northwest Frontier and Balochistan. Education in Pakistan under the best of circumstances was difficult to deliver outside the main cities, one reason being the variation in population density, from roughly 13 people per kilometer in Balochistan to 230 in the Punjab. In the two lowest literacy provinces, Balochistan and Northwest Frontier Province (NWFP), in the 1980s there were roughly 9,000 and 8,000 villages, respectively, with 200 or more people in each and many more settlements with smaller numbers where it was impractical to provide costly buildings and a teaching staff. Geography also made service delivery difficult, from the impenetrable mountainous areas of northern NWFP to the vast deserts of Balochistan.

The population of Pakistan is 97 percent Muslim, but consists of a number of ethnic groups with their own languages: Punjabis (63 percent), Sindhis (12 percent), Pashtuns (16 percent), Baloch (5 percent), and a number of smaller groups. Urdu, considered the language of the elites, was brought from India and used as the language of instruction in Pakistani schools and as a lingua franca among groups in the society. Command of English and Urdu was necessary to obtain employment in the civil service. However only about 8 percent of the population speaks Urdu as a mother tongue, and rural children—especially girls—are rarely exposed to either Urdu or English. The line between those who speak English well and those who do not is a defining feature of class in Pakistan (as it is in Egypt) and tends to depend on whether a child has attended a government or a private school.[2]

In the late 1980s and early 1990s when USAID provided assistance to the education sector the proportion of the Pakistan's expenditure on primary education was 1.5 percent of GNP (in 1980) and it rose to 2.3 percent (in 1991). These numbers are exceedingly low considering that UNESCO recommends an expenditure of 4 percent of GNP.

There were essentially two systems of education operating in parallel: traditional and modern. Modern education in the 1980s was delivered through four systems:

- Government schools that accounted for about 80 percent of students across the country and virtually all students in rural areas;
- Local government systems operating in key urban areas;
- Private schools, which adhered to the federal curriculum but could add subject matter and improve on existing course materials; and
- *Madrasa* or mosque schools with government-appointed teachers to teach core subjects of the federal curriculum.[3]

The Ministry of Education (MOE) in Islamabad oversees primary education and formulates policy. The provinces are responsible for delivering education, but have varying administrative structures to do so. There are twelve grades of formal schooling, divided into four stages:

1. primary (grades ones through five),
2. middle (grades six through eight),
3. intermediate (grades nine through ten), and
4. secondary (grades eleven through twelve).

In some areas, all 12 grades are housed in one school, while in others, one stage or possibly two are located in a single school. Most primary schools in the 1980s had an unofficial "*Kachi*" class of preschool children that sometimes was included in enrollment counts and sometimes not. In some provinces, schools with more than one stage were supervised by separate administrative units with separate budgets.

The Pakistani constitution states that primary education is a right of every child, but it was impossible in the 1980s to enforce compulsory primary education because there simply weren't enough schools and classrooms to meet the need.

ISSUES REQUIRING DONOR ASSISTANCE IN PAKISTAN

The three main issues at the primary level in the late 1980s and early 1990s were as follows:

- Low literacy rates and enrollments, especially for girls and rural children;
- Poor academic quality in government primary programs; and
- Poor management capacity in the education sector.

Issue One: Low Literacy Rates and Enrollments, Especially for Girls and Rural Children

Although census figures were unreliable in the 1980s, Pakistan without a doubt had one of the lowest literacy rates in the world outside of Africa.[4] The gender gap was the second highest in the world[5] and grew wider between 1985 and 1995. Census figures however still remained too unreliable to determine the precise proportion of school-age children out of school and therefore figures of any sort were only rough estimates.

By the start of the official USAID program in 1990 there were 128,000 schools in Pakistan with 8.9 million children enrolled. Household surveys[6] (see table 4.1) reported that only 71 percent of age-appropriate boys and 62 percent of girls were in school. Of those who entered, about half completed

Table 4.1 Net (age-appropriate) enrollment (data from the 1990 Pakistan Household Survey)

	Boys (percent)	Girls (percent)
National	71	62
NWFP		
Urban	86	60
Rural	60	38
Balochistan		
Urban	62	38
Rural	62	28

grade five and only a third went on to higher levels. Dropout and repetition rates were especially high in the lower grades (40 percent dropped out and 13 percent repeated Kachi and grade one combined). The two lowest literacy provinces were NWFP and Balochistan, and it was this fact that caused USAID to decide to support education in these provinces.

The lowest enrollment rates in Pakistan were among lower class, rural girls in the provinces of Balochistan and NWFP, the two larger of the four provinces of Pakistan. Those few who enrolled tended to drop out early. In the 1980s female literacy in these areas was reported as low as 5 percent. Middle and upper class urban children were more likely to enroll and remain longer in school, and many whose parents could afford it attended urban private schools to avoid poor quality government programs. Private schools came in all price ranges and qualities.

Community and Family Factors Discouraging Participation and Learning

In the late 1980s, Pakistani officials claimed that the main factors discouraging rural children from enrolling and persisting in primary school were beyond their control. The community and family factors they noted were similar to those found in Egypt: the "ignorance" of parents who could not understand the benefits and were put off by the burdens of education. The officials insisted that these conservative parents would not send their daughters even if opportunities were readily available.

The incentives for boys enrolling were somewhat more attractive since parents viewed education as possibly leading to job opportunities and thereby higher family incomes. By the time however that significant numbers of rural boys graduated in the 1970s and 1980s, the early employment success stories were difficult to replicate. These realities discouraged many parents from sending and keeping their children in school.

For rural girls extended schooling depended more on whether education increased their chances to marry. Some thought educated girls made less desirable wives because they were not as tractable as young illiterate girls. Other families with educated sons felt educated girls would make more companionable wives or in some urban cases believed their work in professional jobs could increase household income. In most cases, though, men insisted upon wives with fewer years of schooling than themselves and as a result the longer a girl stayed in school the smaller her circle of potential suitors became. Her parents were aware that in any case she would contribute work or income to her husband's family after marriage even though her parents had borne the costs of her education. One of those costs was not having her available to work at home. A household survey showed that girls performed roughly 85 percent of the household work in rural areas, and that their contributions became significant at an earlier age than boys. For enrolled girls, house work invariably interfered with attendance, homework, and study for exams. When a parent was sick or died, girls were the first to be removed from school to do the extra work.

Other reasons parents kept girls home were also familiar from Egypt. They included the fear of letting a daughter walk to school alone or the burden of sending a father or brother to accompany her. Parents might insist, as a condition for girls attending school, that they attend sex-segregated facilities with women teachers. Few small communities had single-sex facilities or educated women to teach girls, and there was also the issue of motivation since girls rarely saw educated women role models to inspire them to want to go to school. Also primary schooling was often not taken seriously for girls or boys if middle and higher education stages were not available nearby. Primary schooling alone had little utility in most villages where there were few opportunities to read and little reading material available.

School Factors Affecting Participation

On the supply side there were obvious factors that discouraged participation. The main one was the lack of opportunities. Many villages had no schools, or had ones that were too distant or ones that in practice admitted only one sex. The government discouraged alternative programs—nonformal and informal—by not making it possible for their graduates to progress easily to higher stages of the formal system.

The costs of schooling were also high. Parents provided notebooks, slates, writing materials, in some case uniforms or clothing of a better quality than everyday wear, shoes, and in most cases textbooks.

Issue Two: Poor Academic Quality in Government Primary Programs

International experts and Pakistani government officials generally agreed that the government program failed to teach many of the skills children needed to become productive adults—in particular critical-thinking and problem-solving skills, as well as science and language skills. The majority (roughly two-thirds) of children failed primary school-leaving exams, even though the passing grade (one-third of test items correct) was set artificially low. Rural, poor and girl children[7] were more likely to fail than their urban, middle- and higher-class boy counterparts. The consequence was that a student either had to repeat a grade or drop out, and parents were more likely to push failing sons to continue rather than daughters, especially if the family had limited resources. The high repetition and dropout rates made the average cost of producing a primary school graduate extremely high for the Pakistani Government, while high repetition rates reduced the openings for incoming students and increased crowding in existing classes.

School Factors Discouraging Learning

Children, especially girls, found the schooling environment unpleasant with its harsh discipline,[8] teasing by other students, and rote learning methods. It was an observable fact that teachers in rural coed (where they existed) classes focused on boys, while girls sat at the back of the class and were rarely called upon. Parents in both urban and rural schools usually insisted on female-only facilities by grade four when their daughters reached puberty. But from grade four on in the Pakistani system specialists were required to teach subjects—math, language, social studies, and religion—that were considered too difficult for generalist teachers. Where one female teacher might have been sufficient for the first three grades, by grade four several teachers were needed. As in Egypt when female teachers were assigned to rural schools far from their urban homes, they were frequently absent or came late, and children sat unsupervised much of the time since there were no substitute teachers.

The schooling environment was especially unattractive to young entry-level children where classes in the lower grades typically contained 50 or more students. Crowding and hours of inactivity caused many to drop out and never return to school. Those who stayed found the classes boring or difficult to keep up with.

Textbooks were another problem. To keep costs low books were often limited to a minimum number of pages (16 to 32) and unless creatively elaborated by a teacher were inadequate for studying a whole year of a subject. The early primers for example skipped from alphabet letters to paragraphs of writing with no transitional decoding exercises. "Tricky" exam questions soon weeded out those who did not master the memory skills needed to succeed. Parents often were unwilling to invest further in these "academically weaker" children, simply saying they "didn't take to schooling."

Urdu posed a special problem for children not previously exposed to the language, especially since Urdu textbooks were not written with adequate regard for the fact that it was a second language for most. Compounding the problem was religious instruction that required children from a young age to learn phrases and sayings from the Koran in Arabic, another foreign language for them. Finally English, a language so essential to civil service jobs, was barely taught in rural schools because most teachers didn't know the essentials of the language.

Overall, as in Egypt, rural parents saw few rewards and many burdens in educating children. Government schools produced graduates who were so poorly prepared that they could not compete with private school graduates for university slots, civil service employment, or private-sector jobs. Nor did these graduates feel comfortable any longer pursuing the manual occupations of rural life.

Issue Three: Poor Management Capacity in the Education Sector

There was a litany of factors widely known to Pakistanis that contributed to the mismanagement of the education system. And it was not long before they also became well-known to the consultants working on the USAID project. Despite the discouraging picture they give, it is important to describe them since they became the major challenges of the reform efforts.

Lack of Sustained Political Will at the Top

One of the important problems was the lack of sustained political will to support reform. As political appointees, ministers of education rarely stayed long in their positions, and often were more interested in the political visibility of the job than in taking on the difficult challenges of reform. In any case it was difficult to wield authority over the entrenched independent-minded bureaucracies of the provinces. It was a common practice when ministers came to power to discontinue the programs of their predecessors so they could make their own mark with visible new programs. Although highly educated themselves—often as doctors or lawyers—these ministers rarely had any background in managing programs or understanding the learning needs of children.

Poor Coordination of the Education Sector

Another major challenge was the lack of coordination among the critical elements in the education system: its national goals, stated learning objectives, teacher training programs, instructional materials, exams, and supervisory systems. Each of these elements operated virtually independently of one another. In addition most had federal and provincial branches with overlapping functions and no clear mandate for their operations. Each could refer decisions to the other as, for example, when a provincial branch claimed that inflexible mandates from the federal level prevented them from addressing known problems.[9]

Lack of an Effective Provincial Structure

The provincial management structure was a problem for any program trying to reform the primary level. Its organization into a tight one through 12 administrative system allowed disproportionate attention and funding to be focused on the upper secondary stages despite the much smaller numbers of students enrolled at that level.

Weak District Management

District Education Officers (DEOs) were another weak link. They saw their role not as managers of reform but as gatekeepers over appointments and transfers in a patronage system that benefitted them. They appointed outsider staff to village schools, for example, in part to minimize the challenges insiders might mount with the support of their own local communities. Their control over school admissions, job appointments, and even exam scores gave the DEOs lucrative opportunities to promote themselves.

Rampant Corruption

One outcome of provincial and district officers' control was that rampant corruption existed throughout the system. Most transactions required a bribe—sometimes a whole year's salary to become a teacher or staff member—and consequently large numbers of "paper schools," and "ghost teachers and supervisors" drained resources from the system. Unqualified candidates for teaching positions took precedence over qualified applicants if their bribe was higher. Wherever an official was a gatekeeper for something people wanted, she or he was invariably taking the opportunity to benefit personally.

The "culture of corruption" influenced officials' perceptions of what was important in the system—mainly material goods and commodities that provided better opportunities for graft. Less important were intangibles like quality improvements. This view carried over into attempts to control every aspect of the education system, including the imposition of rules about school construction, qualifying teachers, or dispensing diplomas where they could be tough or flexible depending on what could be gained. In turn official rules were created to cut down on this abuse, and they created a whole new layer of inflexibility, without achieving their goal. This rigidity instead discouraged alternatives for delivering education to areas where meeting the formal requirements of proper schools and qualified teachers was too costly.

Lack of Accountability

The system as a whole lacked accountability. There were virtually no penalties for the poor performance of teachers, principals, and supervisors. Although for example in extreme cases there was recourse to the courts for abuses, no one dared to turn whistleblower since they were either involved in similar activities or could be made to look as if they were.

Government-wide civil service regulations and automatic promotion rules based on seniority discouraged teachers and administrators from taking initiatives or assuming responsibility for results. Service rules were contradictory, not collected in a single place for reference, and consequently were ignored or not accurately implemented. Some rules simply became a matter of practice and it was not clear where they were recorded.

Chronic Underfunding

Certain elements of the education system were chronically underfunded. For example, rural schools rarely met even minimal standards even though at some time they must have been recorded as meeting the sector standards. Most had no latrines, running water, heating, or electricity. Windows were often broken, the walls chipped, dirty, and unpainted. Many rural buildings were so insecure that nothing could be kept safely in them after school hours. At the same time most schools had costly perimeter walls surrounding them.

Perhaps more important for the program itself was the absence of sufficient resources for the travel expenses of supervisors, who were supposed to be the backbone of quality control. As a result they frequently visited urban schools near their offices but rarely travelled to rural schools farther away. When they did make school visits, they spent most of the time filling in forms that had little to do with teaching and learning: the orderliness of school facilities and grounds, inventories of furnishings, teachers' attendance, and lists of teacher characteristics believed to make them good at teaching.[10] Actual observations of teachers were rare, and at best supervisors asked students to recite short passages to find out if they had progressed to the point in the book that was officially mandated in the schedule by that date.

Resistance to Quality Reforms

Textbooks that formed the basis for student memory work were written by specialist professors in areas of their expertise. Most knew little about child development and chose topics and wordings that were often difficult for young children. For example, the math curriculum started with the concept "null." The textbooks were never evaluated for their effectiveness before dissemination across the province. The writers and the distributors of the books resisted textbook reforms and giving free books to school children because of the profits they gained from their sales.

Because of this control it was difficult to improve the instructional quality of books. "Experimental" books were allowed but they could not become official until the Curriculum Bureau in Islamabad approved them and since officials there stood with the professors, it was impossible to get them to acknowledge that new books might be improvements over the old ones, even when there was clear evidence that children were learning better with the new books. Provincial officials understood the futility of trying to make reforms even if they had felt it was in their best interest to do so. Getting federal approval was close to impossible.

Ineffective Teacher Training

Teacher training was another problem. Teachers were trained according to a formal curriculum that emphasized methods for teaching in normal size classrooms under optimal Pakistani conditions. Teachers were expected to have already mastered the subject content of the primary curriculum (although many had not), and they were not taught standard concepts about learning, such as engaged instructional time, critical-thinking skills, or the need for children to practice new concepts independently. Teachers of large, small, or multigrade classes all were trained to use the same methods—"lecture method," "play-way method," and so on, but when reaching the classroom immediately reverted to the rote methods they had experienced as children, largely because "innovative" methods were hard to implement under the existing conditions in classrooms.

The Effect of Exams

School staff taught to the exams—as they do everywhere—which meant making sure children memorized as much of the textbook as possible. Teachers were not exposed to the idea of "academic skills or competencies," other than as the general "ability to read, write and do math." Test items were not constructed to identify specific learning deficits: for example, a single math item might require several types of computation, making it impossible to determine which of the skills the children lacked when they answered incorrectly.

Inadequate Measures of Progress

Managers could not depend on the reliability of school data for planning. Statistics on enrollments, attendance, and dropouts were routinely falsified to acquire more funding for a school or they were prepared inconsistently so they could not be compared across schools. School principals laboriously filled in multiple overlapping forms that asked for the same data. Measures of quality if anyone had wanted to use them were the inexact proxies of pass rates, student-teacher ratios, or class size rather than measures of actual student skills. Once collected, data were virtually impossible to retrieve from piles of handwritten ledgers stored in warehouses and closets.

DONOR CONSIDERATIONS IN SUPPORTING ASSISTANCE[11]

In the areas where it provided education assistance in the 1980s, USAID's education policy was focused on increasing the availability of formal education opportunities for children of ages six to fourteen, particularly for girls and the rural poor. In addition the policy supported attention to system efficiencies, and coordination with host governments and other donors.

Additional policy guidance came in the form of the 1988 and 1989 Foreign Assistance Appropriations Bills. The 1988 legislation added an amendment that not less than 30 percent of funds appropriated for education programs must be used for programs to reduce illiteracy and that they must tailor basic education to the needs of the poor (especially at the primary level) through reforms of curricula, teaching methods, and improved teacher training. In 1989, 50 percent of the education account ($67.7 million that year) was earmarked for basic education, with South Asia identified as one of two priority geographic areas. Congressional support particularly prioritized increasing educational opportunities for girls.

The United States saw Pakistan as a vital ally during the Cold War, and especially following the Soviet Union's invasion of Afghanistan in 1979 when South Asia became central to US efforts to counter communism. Large amounts of US military and economic aid flowed to Pakistan, both to bolster Pakistan's economy and military and to support Afghan refugees living in Pakistan as well as the cross-border "freedom fighters" operating out of Pakistan. Reflecting the special strategic relationship with Pakistan, USAID decided that dollar funds could be used by Pakistan's federal government as it wanted (most went to pay off debt) as long as a corresponding amount of rupees was set aside for the education budgets of the two provinces USAID designated for its assistance. Those rupees would be released to the provinces by the Ministry of Finance when USAID agreed, in consultation with officials in the provinces and technical assistance teams that policies had been changed, procedures improved, and commitments made to try new approaches. In short, the release of the funds was staged to match progress in both provinces, and decisions about funding bypassed the federal MOE.

The Program: Assistance to Pakistan Education (1987 to 1994)

USAID support for the Pakistan education sector began in 1987 and lasted until the summer of 1994. The Pakistan Education Development (PED) Program had roughly four phases:

1. An initial study period to gather information on the education sector;
2. A design phase that resulted in recommendations by consultants, a reworking of their proposals by USAID, and lengthy consultation between designers and provincial education officials to plan the milestones, activities, and work plans for the program;
3. An implementation phase that lasted from 1990 through 1993 when the program was suspended for political reasons; and
4. A brief drawdown phase during the first half of 1994.

Phase One: The Study Phase

BRIDGES (Basic Research and Implementation in DevelopinG Education Systems) Studies

Starting in 1987 a consortium of universities (the BRIDGES Project) managed under Harvard's Institute for International Development conducted studies in seven countries including Pakistan to prepare for possible USAID support for education. In Pakistan BRIDGES conducted three studies in collaboration with researchers from the Academy for Education Planning and Management in Islamabad:

- a quantitative study of 500 government schools;
- an intensive qualitative study in a small number of classrooms; and
- a "mosque school" study.

The aim of the quantitative study was to identify education inputs that increased student learning while the qualitative classroom study sought to identify effective teaching/learning practices in classes of 32 "good" and "poor" schools selected by local supervisors. Academic skill tests were administered to children in the first and second studies and inputs and teaching practices were correlated with the results. The mosque school study aimed to understand conditions in mosque schools to see if they might provide an alternative to formal schools in certain areas.

Results of the Quantitative School Studies

Student scores from exams administered in the study schools overall were exceedingly poor, and few of the "educational inputs" showed significant impact on learning. The important findings were as follows:

- The more years of *academic* training the teachers completed, the better their students performed;
- Whether teachers were *professionally* trained in teacher training institutes or not made no difference in student performance;

- Rural students of female teachers performed more poorly than students in urban areas or with male teachers;
- Students who understood the language of instruction, or had lessons translated for them, performed better (the language of instruction was not the mother tongue of most children).

Results of the Qualitative Classroom Studies

The intensive qualitative studies of classroom teaching and learning showed the following:

- Students performed better on skill-based exams when teachers augmented rote memorization with other methods (although the norm was memorization).
- Students performed better when teachers added extra steps to their instruction, and the more steps they added the better the children performed.
- Students performed better when teachers required more variety in the way the students practiced new concepts.
- Classroom management—such as the way children were arranged in the class or the order in which they were called upon to recite—affected their learning.

Overall the more the teachers incorporated "effective" teaching steps into their instruction the better students did on the skill-based exams. The steps were identified as follows:

1. explaining what students should learn from a lesson;
2. clarifying new concepts with examples;
3. guiding students initially in the practice of the new concepts;
4. assigning independent practice (seatwork or homework);
5. assessing students' acquisition of skills at the end of the lesson; and
6. holding periodic reviews of previous work.

These steps—sometimes known as "direct teaching"—were later incorporated into a lesson format for textbooks developed under the USAID PED program.

Results of the Mosque School Study

In 1978/9 the MOE had instituted a Mosque School Policy that allowed mosques to be used as schools between prayer calls. The MOE assigned qualified teachers to teach the normal primary curriculum in a three-year time frame, and gave imams a stipend to teach religion. The study examined the factors that might attract or discourage girls' participation in these schools, and tried to determine if this strategy for increasing girls' participation worked. The study concluded that

- the schools did increase girls' participation (measured against whether they were likely to have been in school at all);
- there were wide variations in impact on participation with the highest in Sind and the lowest in NWFP;
- girls were more likely to go to a mosque school if it was located within a kilometer of their homes, and unlikely to go if it was further;
- if a government school was within this one kilometer radius it was preferred over the mosque school;
- more girls went to the schools when the imam supported girls' education; and
- other factors did not appear to have a significant impact on girls' participation.

Other Findings of the Studies

Papers based on data from these studies showed that students in multigrade classes generally performed more poorly on tests than students in single-grade classes and that women primary teachers approached teaching in more interactive ways than men teachers who were more inclined to lecture. One paper looking at the education system as a whole found that there was virtually no alignment among textbooks, teacher training, and exams, nor did these elements in any way link up with federal curriculum goals.

Disseminating the Findings

BRIDGES senior researchers toured provincial capitals presenting the study findings to education officials. Only lower-level education officials attended the sessions, and showed little interest in the information. The BRIDGES researchers concluded that study findings were not an important basis for policy reform in Pakistan—that most Pakistanis considered studies unreliable and intentionally distorted to support their authors' biases. Indeed, a few months after the findings were disseminated the government enacted a policy that gave priority to appointing teachers with professional qualifications rather than those with longer academic but no professional training, ignoring the BRIDGES findings that showed the former to be less effective.

Lessons from the BRIDGES Studies

At the very least these field studies gave foreign and Pakistani participants a more realistic view of what was happening in schools. The studies in retrospect may have combined too many objectives—to acquire useful data for planning the assistance, to develop local research capacity, to conduct reliable studies, and to use a relatively new and difficult analytical tool that eventually had to be used mainly by US graduate students.[12] The generally weak work ethic, lack of interest, and inadequate research skills of many of the local researchers made it difficult to complete studies with the rigor BRIDGES had hoped to achieve in the time frame it had available. For those reasons the research largely failed as a training exercise for Pakistanis, although it produced a better understanding of the conditions in which the assistance would take place.

Phase Two: The Design Phase for US Assistance

The design phase was conducted in three steps:

1. A preliminary design was recommended by a team of technical experts;
2. USAID proposed a support program for Pakistan; and
3. USAID-contracted consultants and Pakistani officials together developed an action plan.

Preliminary Design

Armed with the information from the BRIDGES studies and their previous experiences in assistance projects, a team of largely US technical experts contracted by USAID gathered in Islamabad to lay out the preliminary needs for US support for Pakistan. The team proposed activities to address widely recognized problems in the Pakistani education sector and the specific deficiencies identified in the BRIDGES studies. They assigned levels of effort and estimates of costs to the activities.

USAID's Proposed Program

USAID/Washington refined these initial proposals into a Request for a Proposal (RFP) outlining the scope of an education support program. The main goals of PED were to increase primary enrollments with a special emphasis on girls and rural children and to improve the quality of the academic program in the two low-literacy provinces of Balochistan and NWFP. The PED program was to be funded for ten years with a $280 million dollar grant, of which 80 percent was to go to school construction and smaller amounts for textbook development, training, and other activities to improve the quality of the academic program. Consulting companies submitted proposals detailing how they would implement such a program, identifying the staff they would use, and how much it would cost. Eventually a consortium of educational institutions and companies won the bid and began the work.

The "program" approach proposed by USAID was unique at a time when "projects" were the common vehicle for donor support. The program approach required Pakistanis and USAID consultants to collaborate in setting the goals, in detailing activities to meet them, and in identifying the annual milestones that would trigger each new tranche of money. USAID hoped these milestones would motivate Pakistani officials to reform their institutions to make them more efficient at achieving the results. In theory this approach put Pakistanis in charge of their own reforms even while expecting them to use foreign consultants to shape the changes that would be necessary to trigger the next amounts of money.[13]

Collaborative Planning
A team of US consultants spent a month each with Pakistani officials in NWFP and Balochistan Province planning their respective activities. Initially the Americans and the Pakistanis were far apart in their expectations of how USAID money would be used. The Americans talked about increasing girls' enrollments and improving quality, the Pakistanis talked about the need for buildings, cars for officials, motor bikes for supervisors and furnishings for schools. In both provinces local officials equated "quality" with the sturdiness of buildings or the technical specifications of commodities. Hot topics included whether costly "walls around schools" were necessary, how many cars should be purchased for provincial and district offices, and whether desks were needed for all classes (younger children typically sat on the floor and desks took up space needed to accommodate them).

Nevertheless the consultation period eventually came to an end with a report mapping out the reforms that would occur over the ten-year program and the annual milestones that would signal USAID's release of the following year's funding.

Phase Three: The Implementation Phase in NWFP (1990–1994)

The US consultants kicked off the program with a week-long workshop in Abbottabad on educational research for DEOs from Balochistan and NWFP. The intent was twofold: for the foreign consultants to become acquainted with the DEOs who would play a major role in the program, and for DEOs to see how evidence-based research could play a role in policy making.

After the workshop the foreign consultants split into two teams with each focusing on a province. *The remainder of this case study deals with PED activities in NWFP.* To simplify the description, the activities addressing the three main objectives of the program are described separately, even though in actual practice all three took place simultaneously.

Objective One: Increasing Enrollments in NWFP
The activities to increase enrollments were targeted at rural children and girls who were the largest out-of-school group. Four activities supported this goal.

- Creating a policy climate to encourage the enrollment of girls;
- Increasing schooling opportunities in rural areas, especially for girls;
- Assessing the obstacles to girls' education; and
- Increasing the number of rural female teachers.

Unexpectedly another PED activity encouraged rural enrollments to rise significantly: the provision of free experimental textbooks (see below).

Creating a Policy Climate to Encourage the Enrollment of Girls
USAID and Pakistani officials agreed at the start of the program that schools built in NWFP with US money would be constructed in a ratio of 60:40, with more girls' schools than boys' schools. At the time, most schools were designated either for boys or girls unless they were small multigrade rural schools, or schools where related neighborhood children enrolled and the teacher was a trusted member of the community. It was felt that building a proportionately larger number of girls' schools would help right the imbalance in opportunities open to them, without precluding the possibility of also providing schools for boys where these were needed. Some communities however complained about the "undue emphasis" on girls when PED built girls' schools and boys had to go to crowded or distant schools.

Increasing Schooling Opportunities for Girls

At the start of the PED program it was estimated that 21 percent of rural girls and 9 percent of rural boys did not have an appropriate school available within a kilometer of their homes. Consequently USAID saw school buildings as a priority in increasing enrollments[14] even though no precise information existed at the time on where schools were needed or even where they were located. PED's construction activity, similar to that in Egypt, was handled by a separate contract to ensure the appropriateness of the locations, the suitability of donated plots, and the quality of the construction.

Assessing the Obstacles to Girls' Education

During the planning stages provincial officials were pessimistic about the prospects for increasing girls' enrollments because they believed parents were too conservative to send their daughters, it was too difficult to find female teachers, and land was too costly to procure for schools. Moreover if parents insisted on single-sex schools it would be too costly to build a second school in every settlement. Parents' attitudes about girls' education therefore became an important policy issue with cost implications.

With financial support from UNICEF and USAID, one of the USAID consultants supervised the implementation of a Human Resource Survey (HRS) to determine the extent of these obstacles. The Survey canvassed 8,763 villages in NWFP (and 9,003 in Balochistan) using teachers and supervisors to interview parents and community leaders.

The Survey identified the location of existing schools, their state of repair, and the availability of free land in villages where schools were needed. Interviewers asked leaders and parents if educated local males and females were available to teach school, and whether parents would enroll girls if opportunities existed.

The Survey found that the problem of low enrollment turned out to be less a matter of parental resistance and more about the lack of schooling opportunities for girls.[15]

Parents were considerably more flexible about sending girls to coed schools than officials had reported. A majority said they would send them to coed schools up to grade three and would allow them to study under trusted older male teachers from the local area if female teachers were not available.

Other findings of the Survey in NWFP were as follows:

- In 60 percent of villages more than half the parents claimed they wanted to educate their daughters.
- In 75 percent of the villages schooling opportunities already existed for boys and in 58 percent for girls.
- In villages where girls were enrolled, 58 percent attended "boys" schools while 42 percent attended "girls-only" schools.
- 21 percent of villages claimed that academically qualified females lived either in their village or in a nearby village and could teach the girls.
- Only 4 percent of villages had a "girls" middle school where girls could continue their educations. Nevertheless, in 36 percent of the villages, some girls were attending distant middle schools, compared with 89 percent of villages in which some boys attended middle schools nearby or elsewhere.
- In many cases communities were willing to make land immediately available for school construction.

These findings suggested a more optimistic picture for girls' education than officials were reporting. Parents claimed interest in girls' education and local resources appeared to be available at many sites to increase opportunities quickly. But bureaucratic lethargy, favoritism, and cumbersome procedures in the education department combined to minimize the actual use of the Survey data. In addition, the distrust of research may also have contributed to the failure to use this data effectively.

Increasing the Number of Rural Female Teachers

In NWFP the lack of qualified female teachers was an important constraint on girls' enrollments in rural areas, yet officials refused to modify the requirement that candidates needed a teacher training certificate to be accepted as teachers. Entrance to teacher training institutes however was based on exam scores that favored applicants from better quality urban schools and few rural women qualified. USAID convinced officials to give preferential treatment to rural women who would agree to teach in rural schools, and diverted part of the school construction money to building dormitories next to training institutes where rural candidates could stay during the school year. The fact that rural teachers were paid lower salaries, however, continued to deter recruitment, and eventually an additional small hardship allowance was provided for urban teachers who would teach in rural areas. As with any civil service-related idea, there was considerable reluctance to make a change that might affect budgets and staff in other government sectors.

Providing Free Experimental Textbooks

As the PED program progressed, experimental textbooks came on line for testing in the lower primary grades. Each year the number of schools receiving free experimental textbooks increased. Normally parents paid for textbooks in NWFP and the sudden availability of free books through the PED program led to an unexpected surge in enrollments in the experimental schools, suggesting that a policy of free textbooks for rural children might have had a major impact on enrollments, at far less cost than buildings. Balochistan already provided free textbooks for rural children but NWFP refused, officials said, for budgetary reasons.

Other Contributions to Increasing Enrollments

At the time, a number of other organizations and donors were also active in the education sector of Pakistan including the World Bank, UNICEF, the German Government's GTZ, and a number of INGOs and NGOs. The USAID project however was implemented largely independent of these other projects that tended to be focused on certain beneficiaries or on improving limited aspects of the program.

As noted above the Government of Pakistan (GOP) implemented programs to increase enrollments. Its initiatives included the 1978/9 policy (see above) that allowed mosques to be used as schools. The mosque school program was estimated to have enrolled 630,000 students, of which 30 percent were girls. By the 1990s however the schools were closed, largely because education officials said they didn't meet the formal criteria for primary schools and therefore had to be inferior. Education officials expressed discomfort with the independence of these schools.

A similar nonformal system of "drop-in schools" (Nai Roshni) was instituted for ten- to fourteen-year old dropouts using government schools after regular hours, but the program again met the disfavor of education officials who disapproved of programs operating outside formal requirements. In addition local school officials feared they would be held responsible for any damage caused to the facilities by the drop-ins.

UNICEF supported an NGO project to provide community schools based on the Bangladesh BRAC model, and while these schools demonstrated a better than usual education for children, graduates had difficulty entering higher levels of the formal system because of bureaucratic antipathy to nonformal programs and their reluctance to recognize the credits of their graduates. UNICEF worried that the program could not be sustained if graduates could not move to higher stages.

Another major initiative was supported with a $64 million loan from the Asian Development Bank. A main component of that project was construction of 980 community schools for girls built on a single model of 5 classrooms, administrative offices, toilets, and drinking water facilities. In the first phase, only 40 percent of the target schools were completed and many of these schools stood empty or partially empty because communities either did not have enough students to fill them or teachers could not be found to staff them. Eventually Pakistan would need to pay back the loan, further contributing to its debt load.

A World Bank project hoping to attract female teachers to rural areas built 320 residences across Pakistan so female teachers could live in settlements near their place of work, but these were not acceptable for cultural reasons—female teachers simply did not feel comfortable living away from the protection of male relatives. Most of the hostels were converted for other purposes.

The lack of bathroom facilities and the cost of supplies were other well-known obstacles to girls' enrollment. Overall in Pakistan in the 1990s, it was estimated that 73 percent of schools did not have toilet facilities, 68 percent did not have safe drinking water, and 73 percent had no electricity. Donors responded by building latrines, providing drinking water, and handing out free school supplies. While the improved facilities helped, only a small number of schools benefitted in this way because of limited funds. Other donors handed out school kits with teaching materials to make learning more concrete but they proved largely superfluous in the context of rote learning despite training for teachers in how to use them.

Objective Two: Improving Program Quality in NWFP

The activities to improve education quality focused on increasing student learning of academic skills. In Pakistan these skills were already defined in the stated goals and learning objectives of the Pakistani Government but had not been specifically linked to other program inputs. Six PED activity areas supported these goals.

- Determining the needs and conditions for improving quality;
- Preparing a user-friendly curriculum;
- Installing quality components and focusing them on student learning;
- Evaluating the effectiveness of new components;
- Improving teacher capacities; and
- Mounting an effective English program.

Determining the Needs and Conditions for Improving Quality

The first PED activity—the workshop for DEOs from Balochistan and NWFP—highlighted research as a basis for education decision making. Near the end of the week in Abbottabad the participants conducted a small study of instructional time in multigrade and single-grade classes. They developed observational forms and applied them in the two kinds of classrooms. The results showed clearly that students in single-grade classes spent considerably more time actively engaged in learning than their counterparts in multigrade classes. The participants "brainstormed" how teachers in multigrade classes might keep children engaged in learning more of the time. One suggestion was to assign them "contingent tasks" when teachers turned their attention to other students, meaning tasks that required clear evidence of being completed, such as written exercises. While some participants were impressed with the data that came from the brief study, the training did not wholly reverse the years of distrust in research results.

Another early activity brought together consultants and district supervisors to study the classroom conditions in NWFP relevant to textbook reforms. The act of involving supervisors in determining needs was aimed at sensitizing them to the reasons for the reforms they would later implement. Although their duties presumably gave them an intimate knowledge of schools, many supervisors in fact knew little about instructional practices in classrooms. The study found that the textbooks would have to be fairly self-evident if teachers were to use new methods effectively. Most teachers only knew rote teaching methods, were faced with crowded classrooms, and had few if any additional resources to use even if they had wanted to try something new. A common practice of the teachers was to appoint students to lead choruses of times tables but without any attempt to determine if the students absorbed this information. The books would also need clear learning objectives so teachers would be aware of what it was that they should be teaching.

Preparing a User-Friendly Curriculum

The PED curriculum consultant started her activities by approaching the director of the NWFP Curriculum Bureau in Abbottabad so they could coordinate their efforts on textbook reform. The Bureau was located at some distance from the Directorate of Primary Education in Peshawar, and there was little communication between them. The Bureau director refused to move the Bureau to Peshawar but eventually agreed to let PED establish a small instructional materials center next to the primary directorate in Peshawar. This new Instructional Materials Development Center (IMDC) advertised in the newspaper for young primary school teachers with university degrees to apply for positions as textbook writers.[16] To select the best of the applicants the IMDC director held a workshop where she asked them to show how they would demonstrate abstract concepts to young children using concrete examples.[17] At the end of the workshop she chose a dozen young men and women to join the IMDC.

The specialist and her writers began by preparing a curriculum plan that laid out the learning objectives in math and language arts in sequential order for the primary grades.[18] Next they prepared a lesson format that would be used consistently throughout the textbooks. The format followed the “effective teaching steps” identified in the BRIDGES’ research (see above). Once a teacher understood the format there would be no need for further training unless her students’ results showed she needed more help in learning the format. The writers prepared the textbooks in Urdu and Pashto and year by year new books were added for higher grades in the two core areas of math and language arts. Pashto speakers started classes in their mother tongues and then learned Urdu as a second language. Speakers of other languages would begin with Urdu taught as a second language. The self-evident instructions for teachers and the consistent lesson formats made it possible temporarily to bypass the problem of ineffective teacher training. Teachers only needed a short orientation program before using the new books.

Contrary to usual practice in Pakistan, the IMDC textbook writers were asked to avoid specifically religious content even though stories illustrating simple moral points were allowed. The rationale was that other books of the primary curriculum covered topics such as religion and social studies and PED-supported books should focus on core learning skills without getting into sensitive topics that might offend certain communities. The lessons did however include important content such as life skills (first aid, health, nutrition, and science) that provided a way of "loading" more learning into the textbook package. This content however remained secondary to the learning objectives. Care was also taken to make sure the textbooks were free of gender imbalances and stereotypes, and anything that might offend specific ethnic and religious groups.

Installing Quality Improvements and Focusing Them on Student Learning

From the start PED attempted to link all parts of the academic program to student learning. The textbooks were key to developing the linkages. They embedded the federal learning objectives in the consistent lesson formats, and linked these to teacher instructions so even minimally trained teachers could produce better learning in their students. The IMDC prepared simple objective-based tests to evaluate the effectiveness of the books, and the Pakistani writers in the IMDC set high standards (75 percent of items correct) for what they would consider satisfactory learning results. The writers were confident teachers who used the books as directed would generate high exam results in their students.

The testing of the books served the purpose not only of measuring results but in the long run of activating the systems that would support teaching/learning in the province. In the first phase, supervisors from 16 districts of NWFP were trained in the new materials and how to introduce them to teachers. They held workshops in their districts for a small but varied group of Kachi (preschool) teachers and, in subsequent years, for teachers of higher grades. Each year a textbook for a new grade was added in language arts and math, until new textbooks were being used in 750 classes of the province.[19] Every six months supervisors returned to the experimental classes to test the children. If all students in a class did well the teacher simply continued to teach the new material. If most students in a class did poorly the supervisor retrained the teacher in the use of the lesson formats. The PED team felt that once this process of training and testing was repeated again and again over the ten years of the project, it would eventually become an entrenched routine in the same way that ineffective procedures had become routine in the past.[20] Sustainability of the program relied in large part on instilling these routines, with the addition later of a process for identifying problems and making corrections.

Evaluating the Effectiveness of New Components

The IMDC created a small testing and evaluation unit in its offices where staff prepared evaluation forms, trained supervisors in their use, and collected and processed the data. The evaluation of the books had three stated objectives: to make sure the books taught the intended skills, interested children, and were easy for teachers to use. The staff also wanted to make sure they met the same high standards in all schooling environments—urban, rural, boys' schools and girls' schools, large classes and small classes, and multigrade and single-grade classes. Interest and ease of use were assessed through interviews and observations and received high marks.[21] Skills were determined by skill-based tests and in all the contexts but one (Urdu classes in boys' schools of one district where the support system broke down), children met the 75 percent standard IMDC writers set for them. The test results were disaggregated by grade, subject, and teacher to enable supervisors to retrain teachers in specific areas where they were weak. Suddenly with this new learning system, supervisors had a clear way of evaluating teachers' performance even when they were unable to observe them in their classrooms. They could then narrowly focus on those needing help.[22]

Some responded enthusiastically while others resented what they saw as extra work.

For this system to work over the long term, skill-based tests linked to the specific learning objectives were essential. But it took time to convince the federal body responsible for exams to reexamine their testing techniques and develop new skill-based tests. Eventually the director of Primary Education in NWFP, in consultation with the head of the Curriculum Wing in Islamabad, agreed to establish a National Education Assessment Unit (NEAP) in the IMDC offices in Peshawar. NEAP was charged with creating a bank of skill-based test items for Urdu, Pashto, math, and science in grades three through five and determining their reliability as a testing tool in a sample of classes. The exams were intended at this stage not as a test of the individual capacities of children, but rather to see how effectively the newly linked elements in the program were converging in classrooms and producing better learning. Later these tests would have been an effective tool for teachers to know which objectives needed more work or which children needed more help.

Improving Teacher Capacities

The classroom studies conducted early in PED with the supervisors showed additional problems related to teachers. For example, teachers had difficulty managing large classes and seemed unaware of other obstacles to learning such as the considerable time they spent in noninstructional activities like taking attendance. In some classes children sat where they couldn't see the blackboard, or were squeezed three to a desk and could barely write or access the blackboard when called upon. Teachers had few additional instructional materials even of the kind they could easily have made themselves. Some routinely called on certain children while ignoring others, or called children in such a predictable order that the children didn't pay attention until just before their turn came.

The IMDC staff addressed some of these issues by writing a "classroom management" pamphlet outlining the problems and suggesting solutions that had been observed in the classrooms of creative teachers. These creative teachers were invited to the IMDC to demonstrate their ideas, and in one case, where a teacher had designed alphabet blocks to show the three written forms of letters, the IMDC director helped him patent his idea and replicate the blocks for all first-grade classes in NWFP.

During the testing of the new textbooks, it became clear that many teachers also lacked knowledge of many primary-level concepts, and simply skipped over lessons they didn't understand. So IMDC writers prepared booklets that explained math and language arts concepts for the primary grades and provided simple examples. At first they distributed the booklets to teachers in schools but each year the teacher training institutes (TTIs) graduated additional poorly prepared teachers. Unless training changed, it would be hard to maintain high standards for the books in the higher grades.

But TTIs would neither recognize the teacher failings nor change the curriculum they taught. In 1993 IMDC staff talked to the principals of the 18 NWFP TTIs about the problem. The directors rejected these observations as impossible since teacher candidates had all graduated from high schools or universities. IMDC staff convinced the principals to let them test incoming students, explaining that although the principals were convinced the candidates knew content, it would be good to have proof. They reassured the principals that testing would not reflect on the institutes since the candidates were incoming students. With the help of the TTI trainers IMDC staff administered the government's fifth-grade-leaving exam to the candidates, and asked the trainers to score the tests. The results were as IMDC predicted—almost as low as the results of fifth grade students taking the same exam. The tests also showed that the teaching candidates scored lowest in science and math. The women scored about the same as the men on Urdu and science but less well in math.[23] Lengthy in-service experience as a teacher or teaching grade five increased scores overall.

The longer the academic training the better the scores, but on average women had fewer years of academic schooling so were at a disadvantage.

The principals and trainers were alarmed but maintained they could not add content training to their program because "they were mandated to teach method, not content." The IMDC publicized the results by individual training institutes in hopes of motivating them to improve their candidates' knowledge anyway. They gave the trainers the "primary concepts" booklets and told the institute principals that they would return at the end of the school year to retest the students. The scores improved considerably the second time, whether as a result of training in the institute classes or because students studied the pamphlets themselves. IMDC staff planned to repeat the pre- and post-testing each year until it became an established part of the program.

Mounting an Effective English Program

In May 1992, the minister of education requested that PED mount a program to teach English in the fall of the same year. A quick study by IMDC staff determined that English by radio was the only feasible way to teach English since most teachers lacked verbal and written skills in English. A short trial using Kenyan English tapes[24] showed that while younger children had difficulty following the instructions, by grade three they could adequately respond to the cues and instructions of the radio program. The new program (IRI—Interactive Radio Instruction) therefore began at third grade and continued through fifth grade. Pakistan Broadcasting Services taped the short segments that cued children to specific responses using actors speaking with Pakistani accents (as mandated by Pakistani education officials). IMDC staff developed materials to assist reading and writing (with instructions in Urdu for the teachers), and worked with supervisors to distribute the materials and battery-operated radios to participating classrooms. The half-hour lessons were broadcast at scheduled times over the radio. IMDC staff again used supervisors to administer English tests periodically in much the same way the textbook results had been monitored. The children showed they learned the intended vocabulary and short sentences in English. Despite its success, the English program was discontinued when a new minister in 1994 felt languages should be taught by teachers, not radios, and abolished it.

Objective Three: Increasing Management Capacity

PED also aimed to increase the capacity of provincial and district officers to administer the education program effectively. Six activities supported this goal.

- Restructuring the education bureaucracy to separate out and protect financing for primary institutions;
- Conceiving a new role for managers/administrators;
- Instituting policy reforms;
- Improving school statistics and data collection;
- Managing and initiating reforms to increase student learning; and
- Meeting annual program milestones.

Management was the most frustrating area for those hoping to effect a comprehensive overhaul of education in NWFP. Most Pakistani managers achieved their positions through seniority or influence, and not because they were effective administrators. High management posts were desirable in part for the lucrative opportunities they presented,[25] and rarely because a manager wanted to improve the conditions of education. The main managers PED dealt with in NWFP were the Director of Primary Education and the DEOs.

Restructuring the Education Bureaucracy to Protect Primary Education

Before PED began, USAID and NWFP officials agreed that the Directorate of Primary Education should be separated from the bureaucratic structure that administered all preuniversity education. The existing system of combining the levels below the university stage had resulted in a disproportionate amount of resources going to the secondary level. By separating out primary education, USAID hoped to keep its funds concentrated in the lower grades. Unfortunately the split left essential functions outside the control of the new Primary Directorate, including teacher training, the exam bureau, the curriculum unit, and control over supervisory staff. Most of these groups refused to cooperate directly in the reform effort and implementers had to work around their resistance. Eventually some permitted branch offices in Peshawar under the IMDC where they were not involved, but usually well after PED had developed alternative ways of addressing the problem. Leaving these resistant groups uninvolved however meant problems in the future when they would be able to undo or resist entirely important aspects of the reforms.

Conceiving a New Role for Managers/Administrators

The Director of Primary Education and the DEOs as noted saw their role as one of control and patronage. This meant they spent most of their time signing papers (every transfer, record, and purchase), seeing dignitaries, and making highly publicized visits to school ceremonies and provincial events. Engaging such people in the mundane work of running an effective program proved difficult if not impossible. The best that could be hoped was that they would allow reform activities to go on unhindered in their districts.

In an ideal world provincial managers would have championed education reforms and viewed project consultants as allies and adjunct staff. The new Director of Primary Education, who perhaps had the most to gain by making the project a success, and who seemed to have been chosen for his agreeable manner and ability to work with foreign consultants, rarely took any initiative that led to sustained change. His interest lay in maintaining the status quo without so alienating PED consultants that USAID stopped funding the program.[26] When all else failed, he controlled the consultants through bureaucratic means.[27]

DEOs also cooperated only minimally—letting activities take place in their districts but standing aloof from them. Often they would be absent on important business when IMDC staff visited, or would meet with them only briefly.[28] The DEOs too saw their role as exerting control, courting influence, and attending ceremonies, and PED activities annoyed rather than engaged them. The reform activities took their time without enhancing their influence, and since the activities had been mandated by the Directorate in Peshawar, they were essentially beyond the DEOs' control. It was easier for a DEO to absent himself than to respond to the consultants' requests. Conceiving a new role for themselves was not a priority. It was clear the project failed to give adequate attention to "selling" itself to these managers or finding ways to overcome their resistance. But it is also possible that nothing (legal) could have compensated them for the benefits they might lose if the system changed.

Instituting Policy Reforms

Also in an ideal world program needs would have triggered policy reforms. There were some notable successes including the restructuring of the primary directorate and the commitment from the GOP to increase its overall education budget albeit only slightly. Another major success resulted from the "Kachi" study carried out by the IMDC staff and supervisors. In every school they visited they found an informal class of up to 50 or more 3- to 6-year olds. Officials denied the existence of the classes or claimed they were for teachers' children. But when the Pakistani supervisors confirmed that most schools had a "Kachi" preschool class[29] officials reluctantly decided to recognize the classes and promised to provide resources to support them. It was never clear that the resources were made available and in fact funding the classes adequately would have meant adding 25 percent to existing school budgets since the large class consumed at least a quarter of a primary school's classroom space and teachers' time. The important aspect of recognizing the class was that children's ages could be limited, and that the IMDC could officially write age-appropriate textbooks for the class.[30]

Another area where policy reform was needed was in the rules governing teacher performance. Teachers could be absent 25 percent of the time for sickness and "personal" days without penalty, and with no substitute teachers children spent the time sitting unproductively in class. Teachers took advantage of this "absence" rule and other rules that were vaguely recalled but difficult to locate in official documents. PED hired a Pakistani consultant to compile the rules (on absences, promotions, and discipline) in a single volume with the hope of regularizing, possibly reconciling, and eventually reforming them. Unfortunately, although useful as a reference, the manual never led to reforms because PED was discontinued before that could happen. In any case rules that applied throughout the civil service were not easily changed in a single sector. Undoubtedly the ambiguity of the rules served the interests of many in the system.

A policy change that had a detrimental impact on program outcomes was the expansion of "coeducational" schools. In response to community complaints that girls were being favored over boys in the PED building project, provincial officials decided to make all schools in NWFP coed. At first this seemed a victory for girls' enrollments, by giving girls places in boys' schools. But in practice, many parents withdrew their daughters when boys enrolled in girls' schools or when male teachers were hired to teach there. The effect was for many designated girls' schools to become boys' schools. Officials of course blamed the withdrawal of girls on conservative parents and not on their new policy.

Improving School Statistics and Data Collection

Before PED, even if managers had wanted to plan more rationally, statistics were so unreliable it was impossible to know how many schools, teachers, and students existed, their exact locations, or whether enrollments were increasing or decreasing in subsequent years. From early in the program, USAID invested heavily in improving data reliability and use through the following:

- an assessment of existing data collections and storage systems;
- improvements in collection methods and school-level forms; and
- training in computer processing skills, reporting, and, to some degree, in analysis of data.

One difficulty involved irregularities in the way statistics were collected. EMIS (Education Management Information Systems) consultants found for example that schools were categorized as boys' or girls' schools based on the sex of the schools' teachers rather than on the sex of the students. All children in a designated girls' school would be counted as girls. If a boy was enrolled in an early grade of a school with female teachers he would be counted as a girl.[31] From the Pakistani perspective, this seemed logical—since it was a matter of who paid salaries, but the EMIS staff realized that girls were being overcounted as a result. A more detailed reporting form helped solve this problem. In other cases, unclear or differing definitions of what constituted an enrolled student, a dropout, or a repeater made it difficult to keep accurate counts. Some children could be absent for months or even years and still remain on the books as enrolled students while others who were counted as newly enrolled might instead be repeaters.

The time it took to discover these problems and develop new EMIS training systems for data collection, inputting, cleaning, and reporting occupied the limited time available to the EMIS staff. By the time PED ended, EMIS was generating summary reports that were more reliable than previous reports. But deficiencies still remained in the system, the most important being the lack of data analysis and finding a way to connect conclusions to official decision making. Officials made little use of data in planning before, and it was little different when EMIS data came on line. Another serious problem was that EMIS lacked valid indicators of education quality—such as the results of competency-based exams that were available only for the comparatively small sample of IMDC experimental schools.[32] As proxies, EMIS relied on indicators like student/teacher ratios, classroom size, or teacher training[33] even though BRIDGES studies had shown clearly that they had no significant relation to student learning.

Managing and Initiating Reforms to Increase Student Learning

As noted earlier the preparation, distribution, and testing of experimental textbooks provided an ideal opportunity to link the disparate parts of the academic program. This process could also have provided a good opportunity to train managers if they had engaged fully in the activities. It would have given them the opportunity to oversee the development and distribution of innovations and identify components that would be needed to improve results further. With the new managerial tools PED was developing—in the form of EMIS data and learning results—managers would have been able to measure the effectiveness of reforms and could have used them to hold teachers, principals, and supervisors accountable. Moreover PED was training the grassroots developers, data collectors, and implementers who were capable of carrying out the routines that would ensure a quality program. The managers would have been heroes, but this did not happen because PED failed to engage them sufficiently. They continued to stand aloof from the process and although quality components were established without them, their leadership was a critical gap. In the long run, field workers do not operate without direction and financial support from managers.

If PED had not been discontinued, the next steps would have been in-service training for teachers to improve their teaching of competency-based materials[34] and more generally to improve their classroom management skills and content knowledge. The plans were for in-service training to focus first on the practical, concrete needs of local teachers as they and their supervisors identified the needs. The training would ultimately move on to more theoretical understandings of child development and pedagogy as teachers became more engaged. By starting with in-service training, PED consultants hoped to postpone the much needed reform of preservice training where institutional resistance was still very strong. The in-service training would have provided yet another way for DEOs to expand their control since much of the training would be based at the district level and would address local issues.

From the start PED stressed evidence-based decision making and evaluation of the effectiveness of any new innovation. Later in PED if it had continued, the Evaluation Unit in the IMDC would have evolved into a full-scale research and development center to assess problems and test solutions in limited cases before implementing them in the education system as a whole. Once again this expansion would have been an invaluable tool in the hands of active managers. But PED was aborted before that could happen.

Meeting Annual Program Milestones

In the design phase PED consultants and Pakistani educators agreed upon the goals and annual milestones that would trigger the next tranches of funding. These milestones were supposed to motivate Pakistanis to make their own reforms. The idea looked good on paper but without heavy pressure from USAID the Pakistani bureaucracy was difficult to move. Separating out the Directorate of Primary Education proved to be a good milestone but as we have seen, it left relevant units outside the authority of the Primary Directorate, and therefore created an almost insurmountable obstacle to reform. Each year there were additional milestones that were either not met at all or only partially met, while other successes occurred that were not anticipated and in some cases may have been more important than the designated milestones.

Milestones in effect proved to be inexact set of objectives since it was difficult to forecast timelines for activities that were constantly affected by unforeseen events. The milestones encouraged Pakistani officials to tolerate the participation of foreign consultants, whom they saw as virtually guaranteeing them the next tranche of funding. And in fact USAID could not stop or hold back the funds for political reasons,[35] and eventually the Pakistanis realized they had considerable leeway in whether they met the milestones or not. Ironically, the milestones put more pressure on the consultants to bypass resistant Pakistani officials and institutions in order to meet deadlines. On balance the idea seemed good but difficult to implement in practice. Milestones served to underscore the fact that time and money were limited, and without these deadlines it might have been tempting for both sides to avoid the conflicts necessary to move a reluctant bureaucracy.

Phase Four: Draw Down in Four Rather Than Ten Years

The PED Program came to an end in the summer of 1994, less than four years after it started and more than six years before its intended expiration. The Pressler Amendment, adopted in 1985, banned most economic and military assistance to Pakistan unless the President certified annually that "Pakistan does not possess a nuclear explosive device and that the proposed United States assistance program will reduce significantly the risk that Pakistan will possess a nuclear explosive device." In October 1990, President George Bush was no longer willing to issue this certification for Pakistan, which then triggered the Pressler amendment prohibitions and terminated much of USAID assistance to Pakistan over the next few years.[36]

The PED consultants were given six months to suspend activities and work out ways to sustain as many of the positive accomplishments of the program as possible. It was an unfortunate time to suspend activities—in mid-stream before textbooks for grade five were even developed and before the books for earlier grades were finalized. The supervisory support system was just beginning to operate smoothly and more and more supervisors were being included each year in the training and monitoring of the program. Virtually every activity was suspended just as it was beginning to show results but before it became an embedded routine in the education system. In the space of a year after the suspension, little remained of the activities that were showing such important learning results. Once PED was halted, the routines stopped, the books disappeared, and everyone went back to the systems that had existed earlier. Many of the participants had learned new skills but with the structures gone in which to use them, there was no reason to exercise them further.

Lessons from PED

Despite its difficulties, PED was a remarkably successful program while it lasted, and might have transformed education in NWFP if it had run its course and its weaker parts had been strengthened. As the most comprehensive aid program USAID had mounted in the region, PED's lessons are important in informing future assistance efforts. Some of these significant lessons are summarized below.

Successes. A number of aspects of PED were noteworthy. Perhaps the most important was that it pursued the major goals explicitly articulated by the Pakistani Government to increase enrollments of rural children and to improve the quality of education. PED also approached quality issues in terms of the Pakistani Government's detailed learning objectives, focusing much of its assistance on achieving those objectives. That meant approaching education as a comprehensive system, developing effective linkages between instructional inputs, and scrutinizing every element from textbooks to training to exams to supervision and delivery to ensure that it contributed positively to learning outcomes. It meant improving on local approaches and systems rather than trying to introduce approaches that might be incompatible with local ways of doing business. For example, PED used "direct teaching/learning" approaches rather than internationally touted child-centered approaches to move teachers away from rote learning practices. Evidence that these approaches worked was seen in the fact that skill-based test scores increased immediately with the new supportive textbooks.

Other strengths were PED's flexibility, its provision of adequate resources, and its lengthy time frame of ten years. In this framework, participants could work steadily on improving educational inputs where possible, while at the same time considering how they might resolve the unanticipated obstacles hindering reform. For example, PED experts could address the inadequate content knowledge of teachers from several angles: through activities in the TTIs, through clear explanations and instructions in the textbooks, and by indicating explicitly the learning skills that would be tested. This gave time to begin resolving the issue of content knowledge where it was needed in training institutes.

The PED approach was also successful in recognizing the complexity of the elements that make up an education system. The newly developed testing system was a good example of the multiple ways every aspect of a system affects every other part. The test items based on explicit learning objectives were at the same time a motivating force for teachers, measured the successes and weaknesses of the learning program, and acted as a way for supervisors to hold teachers accountable even when they (the supervisors) could not be present to observe them.

Weaknesses. While the approach was well focused and largely effective in the limited duration before the program shut down, there were also a number of weaknesses. One was the modality for channeling resources to PED activities in the provinces. The bilateral government agreements that had called for Pakistan to release local currency equivalents of dollar amounts the United States allotted for PED activities proved an open invitation for Pakistani misuse, and severely slowed the passage of funds to the field. On USAID's side the threat to withhold tranches of money if milestones were not met also proved an ineffective incentive because of political and operational constraints on USAID's ability to withhold funds. The idea seemed good but the means to carry it out were lacking. It is hard, though, to think of a more effective way of motivating Pakistanis to make reforms.

In addition, institutional barriers significantly slowed reform. Separating out the primary bureaucracy proved a good idea in most respects but left essential functions outside the control of the Primary Directorate. Not only were reformers forced to work around these institutions, but they seriously compromised PED's long-term hopes of working through and strengthening existing government structures. After the program started, USAID no longer had the leverage it had in the early stages, and drawing these units more effectively into the reform effort became much harder. Perhaps USAID could have exerted political pressure on higher authorities to make further changes in the bureaucracy but that did not happen. By the time the United States withdrew its support, the reformers had circumvented these problems with ad hoc alternatives. This however did not change the fact that resources and time were wasted in overcoming these obstacles, and existing institutions if anything were weakened rather than strengthened by the reforms.

One reason policy reforms played so little role in facilitating changes was the inherent difficulty in doing anything that limited the authority of line administrators or affected personnel policy that applied to other sectors. Significant changes could only be made when ordered at the highest levels of the Pakistani Government and, in terms of PED program activities, probably only if US negotiators had made policy reforms a prerequisite of funding. Even when consultants and provincial authorities could agree on the need for certain policy reforms neither had the authority to make the changes.

Conventional wisdom stresses the importance of local participation in assistance projects, but there is always a question of how much and what kinds of participation are needed.

A parallel question is what role outside consultants should play. Although PED involved Pakistanis in most aspects of the program, one could argue that too much direction was initiated by the consultants. Without strong direction some of the consultants felt the Pakistanis would simply revert to existing practices, many of which had become the objects of PED reform. Active involvement—for example, in the assessment studies—allowed the Pakistanis to see why reforms made sense, but most did not have the experience or the authority to initiate reforms on their own. Those who participated actively could not make critical decisions, and those who could were unwilling to become involved in "activities below their rank."

PED consultants themselves held significantly different views of their roles in relation to their Pakistani counterparts. Consultants working on management issues felt they were advisors waiting to be consulted, while those working on the grassroots tasks of improving the academic program believed they had to take an activist approach if program goals were ever to be achieved. A great deal of progress was made with this grassroots approach but these successes were difficult to sustain because local managers did not "own" them. Some officials even worked actively against agreements with USAID as when their policy actions turned many of the girls' schools into boys' schools. To be fair, engaging the managers was perhaps the most difficult of PED's tasks since the incentives that might have appealed to many were beyond PED's capacity to deliver.

Essential Lessons from PED Phases

Lessons from the Design Phase

Consultation with provincial officials was intended to be a straightforward effort to plan and establish milestones. It turned out to be more useful in identifying and somewhat narrowing the expectations of Pakistani officials and foreign consultants and donors regarding the nature and scope of the assistance effort. The difference in expectations that surfaced during these meetings however never completely disappeared in the course of implementation.

Lessons from Activities to Increase the Enrollment of Girls and Rural Children

In hindsight enrollments might have increased more rapidly if there had been greater effort on the policy front. The severest constraints on children's enrollments were the rigidity of government rules and procedures regarding school venues, teacher qualifications, and the inability to receive credit outside the formal system. These rules slowed the spread of programs, contributed enormously to costs, and in many cases denied schooling indefinitely to children in small or remote communities. If children had been able to receive credit for demonstrated skills (no matter how they achieved them), there would almost certainly have been a proliferation of nonformal programs sponsored by families, communities, and NGOs. These policy changes would have made it possible to reach more children at less cost than those reached by the small number of new schools that were built by donors. In addition, the unexpected surge of enrollments in experimental schools suggests that providing free textbooks to rural students might have been a policy worth considering.

Lessons from Efforts to Improve Program Quality

PED showed that textbooks could bear a much larger share of the burden of quality improvements than had previously been recognized. The PED books were loaded with elements that eased the reform process and contributed to its successful outcomes while the program lasted: the instructions for teachers, consistent lesson formats to reduce training, systematic approaches to achieving academic skills, and content that included useful life skills. The books overcame resistance to new methods of teaching[37] by embedding direct learning methods into the lesson formats. Testing showed that the new methods worked. An important lesson was that meaningful change in behavior can occur when new approaches are easier for teachers to follow—in this case through consistent lesson formats—than to revert to their old practices. It also proved important that everyone involved saw concrete evidence that learning was improving when they used the new approach.

Lessons from Improving Management Capacities

As already noted, management was the weakest link in the program effort and the most difficult to overcome. Manager positions were highly politicized and their roles already set by tradition as gate keepers and dispensers of favors. PED consultants were unpopular with DEOs largely because they caused additional work and uncovered irregularities that the DEOs depended on to maintain their influence. The fact that the consultants disagreed about their own roles also meant there was never a clear vision for how this problem might be overcome.

Despite Pakistani antipathy to studies and data in planning, PED made important inroads into collecting more reliable school- and teacher-level information. Although not used effectively to locate new schools, the Human Resource Survey also showed for the first time that parents were more willing than previously known to send girls to schools and let them study with boys and male teachers in the early grades. Similarly the involvement of supervisors in classroom and preschool "Kachi" studies made it possible to argue for policy changes and refute official claims that such classes did not exist. As a general rule reforms were more likely to be implemented successfully when Pakistani counterparts helped identify the problems and were involved in finding the solutions to them.

A number of these lessons were useful in informing the next project in Afghanistan even though some of the conditions there were new and challenging, and the lead agency was not USAID, but the multilateral organization UNICEF.

CHAPTER 5

THE AFGHANISTAN CASE: UNICEF AND ITS PARTNERS' SUPPORT FOR PRIMARY EDUCATION (1998–2002)

BACKGROUND

Modern education[1] has a long history in Afghanistan going back to 1868 when the first primary schools opened. In the beginning decades of the twentieth century two pro-Western rulers, Habibullah and Amanullah, expanded the system[2] and brought in foreign teachers. Despite the anti-modern outlook of the next ruler, Nadir Shah, who came to power in 1929, secular education continued and by 1930 there were 13 educational institutions, modeled partially on the French lycee system, with 16,000 students. During this period the government extended primary education to villages across the country that had previously known only mosque schools, and built secondary schools and some teacher training institutes in the main towns. In 1932 Kabul University was established and in the 1950s became coeducational. In the 1920s and 1930s a number of students were given merit scholarships to study in Europe.[3] The 1931 constitution (Article 20) made education compulsory but the lack of facilities in many villages made it impossible to enforce.

The education system continued to grow throughout the next decades of political change as the country went from a period of cautious liberalization in the late 1940s, toward closer relations with the Soviet Union (in the late 1950s), to a constitutional government based on the US and British systems (in 1964), and finally to the overthrow of the king (in 1973) by a leftist member of the royal family who was later killed in a coup. Communist influence grew during the 1970s and the Soviet Union eventually invaded the country in 1979.

Throughout these upheavals, approaches toward education often served as a bellwether of Afghan leaders' vacillating political attitudes—toward the West or toward the Soviet Union. The Soviet Union's occupation of Afghanistan from 1979 until 1989 remains a painful memory in the minds of many Afghans, and still influences their thinking about foreign involvement in the education system.

The Soviets used a regional approach in coopting local populations. In the north they stressed ethnic pride and the cultural commonalities of Afghans with populations in Soviet Central Asia, while in the south (Kandahar) and west (Herat) they carried out bombing campaigns to depopulate the land, ruin irrigation, and destroy villages so people would move to cities where they could be more easily controlled. Most of the education facilities that remained were located in Kabul.

As a means of creating ethnic divisions the Soviets replaced Dari as the lingua franca in schools with textbooks in Pashto, Uzbek, Turkic, and Baloch as well as Dari. Russian replaced other foreign languages and the Soviets hoped it would eventually become the lingua franca for the country. The Soviets did not ban religion but its instruction was significantly reduced and instruction in communist ideology became compulsory. When Afghans resisted the occupation, the Soviets sent more than 50,000 Afghans to the Soviet Union for indoctrination with 20,000 of these children between the ages of four and eight.[4]

A comparison of education infrastructure from the pre-Soviet era (1978) with that at the peak of their occupation (1984) shows the effects of these policies (see table 5.1).

Table 5.1 Afghan schools before and during the Soviet occupation (1978 and 1984)[a]

	1978	1984	% change
Primary schools	1154	210	–82%
Village schools	1451	0*	–100%
Middle schools	350	78	–78%
High schools	163	44	–73%
Technical schools	17	8	–53%
Teacher training	26	6	–78%

Note: * This figure does not include community-supported schools
[a] Adapted from Amin 1987, p. 314.

Over this period from1979 to 1984, tenured faculty also dropped 42 percent from 750 to 432[5] and students by 57 percent from 14,000 to 6,000. So many male faculty and students were killed, jailed, or fled to avoid conscription that classes for a while contained mostly girls.[6] The Soviets claimed that over a million Afghans graduated from literacy courses during their occupation—in 1985, 400,000 were enrolled in these courses.[7]

The Soviets withdrew from Afghanistan between May of 1988 and February 1989 after grooming a procommunist leader Najibullah to take over. But in 1992 after the collapse of the Soviet Union and divisions appeared within branches of the Afghan communist party Najibullah resigned and the Mujahidin (commanders or "freedom fighters") previously living in Pakistan took over the Afghan Government, precipitating a fierce struggle for control. In 1994 a band of intensely religious students, the Taliban, succeeded in overthrowing the Mujahidin Government and in 1996 entered Kabul, after previously taking over the southeastern portions of the country.

CONDITIONS IN THE LATE 1990S AT THE TIME OF THE ASSISTANCE ACTIVITIES

One of the first acts of the Taliban Government in 1996 was to ban female students and teachers from government schools where women comprised 70 percent of the teaching force.

Simultaneously the Taliban withheld funds and supplies from the schools, preferring that the boys attend religious schools where they would be prepared for jihad when they graduated. The Taliban rationale for these actions was that they needed the manpower and resources to complete the conquest of the northern areas. Male teachers were soon forced to augment their incomes with other forms of work including private tutoring and peddling produce on the streets.

During the 1980s when foreign governments (the United States and Pakistan primarily) were supporting the Mujahidin in expelling the Soviets, one area of US assistance had been the development of new textbooks to encourage children and their parents to support the war effort against the Soviets. The University of Nebraska was the prime contractor for USAID in this effort and the result was primary textbooks where virtually every page promoted jihadist war themes. After the Soviets left, and with a few changes in the images, the textbooks were approved by the Taliban for use in Afghan government schools. They welcomed the jihadist message even though the books were weak in pedagogical content.

Afghanistan is 99 percent Muslim,[8] but the population is fragmented into numerous tribes and ethnic groups with their own languages and sense of identity, including Pashtuns, Uzbeks, Tajeks, and Hazaras. The Ministry of Education (MOE) in Kabul oversees the education system and formulates policy. The provinces, through local education offices, take responsibility for delivering education. The system consists of ten grades of formal schooling, divided into two stages: primary (grades one-five), and secondary (grades six-ten). In some urban schools all ten grades are housed in one building, while in others, the stages are located separately. During the Taliban period, although this structure remained the MOE barely functioned.

Problems Requiring International Assistance

What at first had seemed an advantage in Pakistan—a fully functioning institutional structure to deal with education—barely existed in Afghanistan where the government paid little attention to formal schooling. Some international[9] and community groups—especially in the northern areas—took advantage of the lack of oversight to operate virtually undisturbed throughout the Taliban period. But occasionally the Taliban closed nongovernment, clandestinely operated home schools or publicly reprimanded girls for attending programs after grade three. It was therefore difficult to predict the future of these programs even though the schools often reopened after a few weeks with no indication of why they were closed or allowed to reopen.

In Afghanistan there were three main problems in the education system, and although similar in some ways with the problems in Egypt and Pakistan, they were intensified in Afghanistan because of conditions under the Taliban. They were as follows:

- Low literacy rates and limited schooling opportunities;
- Poor academic quality; and
- Difficulties in delivering education.

All these issues were important but the delivery of schooling opportunities was by far the most challenging. How could the international community deliver a quality education to children in Afghanistan without a reliable institutional structure, and do so in a nondiscriminatory way regardless of the children's background or sex?

Low Literacy and Limited Schooling Opportunities

In 1998, when the assistance activities described below were about to start and two years after the Taliban banned females from government schools, primary enrollments were so low and statistics so unreliable that they were no longer officially reported by most international organizations. In 1998 however the UN estimated that roughly 25 million people lived in Afghanistan, including 1.5 million school-age children,[10] and that an additional 1 million lived as refugees in Pakistan, of which 230,000 were school-age children in officially recognized refugee villages.[11] Only 90,000 of these refugee children received an education. Reports in 1997 estimated that literacy rates for Afghan urban men was 35 percent and women 10 percent and for rural men 26 percent and women 3 percent.

An earlier estimate in 1995[12] suggested a much higher figure of roughly 3.8 million children of primary school age[13] living in Afghanistan and of those about a million were enrolled. If that were the actual case it would have taken 10,000 to 20,000 schools to provide education for all Afghan children, yet a 1993 survey reported only 2,200 schools in 28 of the 32 provinces with about half run by international organizations. The majority of those schools were located in cities and large towns.

In 1998 despite the halt in services by a number of education providers due to the Taliban ban on females, there were still 15 Afghan and International NGOs working in 25 of the 32 provinces of the country. The still active agencies were sponsoring roughly 700 boys' schools and 530 girls' schools while the Afghan Government was still running roughly 2,300 schools for boys and 91 for girls.[14] The problem of access was obviously immense despite the lack of reliable statistics.

Poor Academic Quality

With little government oversight in the late 1990s, curriculum and textbooks varied from program to program, along with the relative quality of teaching/learning. A major constraint on quality was the widespread use of the USAID-supported Nebraska textbooks (see above). By 1998 the University of Nebraska press in Peshawar was making the books easily available in the markets where parents bought schoolbooks, and many providers simply found it easier to adopt the books than to develop books of their own. Government schools used modified versions of the Nebraska textbooks approved by Taliban authorities[15] but as noted the books were not written systematically to promote skill development and teachers taught them using rote methods, although efforts were made to train teachers to use them more effectively. Children using these materials took longer to acquire appropriate skills than those using materials developed by other international groups such as the Germans, the Swedes, CARE, and Ockenden International. These internationally produced textbooks were usually better pedagogical tools but they too needed considerable teacher training before they could be used effectively. Under the conditions existing in Afghanistan—including security and travel issues—it was difficult and costly to train teachers adequately even if the environments in their classrooms had supported the new methods.

Another issue was the familiar one of the assistance community focusing its attention on expanding opportunities rather than improving programs. Most educators and staff of international agencies felt "quality" could be achieved simply by training teachers to improve their performance. The foreigners who ran many of the training workshops however often brought in outside perspectives—ideas about pleasant classroom environments and child-centered, hands on manipulative approaches—that were too radical a departure from the usual practices of teachers. The trainers rarely looked to see whether these "creative" approaches actually worked in classrooms. If they had they might have concluded that they were difficult to translate into classroom instruction given crowded classes and existing books and exams that rewarded memorization.

Difficulties in Delivering Education

Afghanistan was perhaps unique at the time in the array of problems affecting the delivery of education. A number of the basic obstacles were simply intrinsic to the conditions of Afghanistan—the difficulty of the terrain, the harsh climate, the multitude of mother tongues, the lack of roads, and the population's resistance to foreign involvement in local schooling. As in Pakistan, conservative parents often saw few benefits and many burdens to sending their children to schools.

Other problems of delivery related to the lack of organizational capacity within the country itself—the lack of government structures and the fragmented nature of international assistance. The destruction of infrastructure caused by decades of war left a number of communities organizing their own informal schools, alone or with the help of Afghan and international NGOs. Many made do with ad hoc venues—mosques, homes, and community halls—and minimally educated teachers. In refugee villages, it was so difficult to find formally qualified female teachers that the responsible international nongovernmental organization (INGO) hired women who had either been home-taught by male relatives or had completed only four or fewer years of schooling. A further difficulty was that many Afghans had lost documents that proved their qualifications, or had their studies so disrupted that it was difficult to know what level of schooling they had completed. Conscientious NGOs administered exams to assess candidates' competence, but like the exams given to children they tested facts and memory rather than skills.[16]

During the Taliban period (from 1996[17] to 2001) and despite their neglect of the education sector, some children still enrolled in home and community schools financed by their parents or the international community. In refugee villages located in Pakistan, Afghan students attended schools organized by Save the Children under the auspices of United Nations High Commissioner for Refugees (UNHCR). Many of these refugee students had fled from rural areas of Afghanistan where education had not been available, and as a result refugee villages offered them opportunities they would not otherwise have had at home. Compared to the difficulties inside Afghanistan, education delivery was often easier in the more densely settled refugee villages, where it was possible to find informal venues and potential (although "less qualified") teachers. By 1998 however Taliban influence was growing in these villages and delivery of services was becoming more difficult, especially for girls. But still refugee demand for schooling was far outstripping the opportunities the assistance community could provide. By contrast, inside Afghanistan, the country was becoming more secure and many refugees were thinking about going back. In an ideal world, graduates of the refugee schools might have jump-started education in rural areas where no schools existed earlier.

The education program in Afghanistan in the late 1990s was a free-for-all. The government neglected education, teachers went unpaid, and enforcement of regulations governing schools was erratic. In the more vibrant nonformal sector supported by local communities and foreign donors, programs were run in whatever manner organizers felt was best. The number of children they enrolled however was limited and confined mostly to certain local areas and the quality of the programs varied from one organization to the next. In short, education during the Taliban period was extremely fluid, opening opportunities at times because of Taliban neglect but also creating hardships when difficult-to-anticipate interruptions occurred. Still, despite these problems demand for schooling was increasing perhaps because people were looking for signs that life was returning to normal after the turbulent period of the Mujahidin.[18]

ACTIVITIES UNDERTAKEN BY UNICEF AND ITS PARTNERS (1998 TO 2002)

This case study presents three examples of actions sponsored by UNICEF and Save the Children/US (SC-US) in Afghan education between 1998 and 2002. While not inclusive of all efforts going on at the time, these examples are illustrative of a range of activities that were. The consultant's roles in these examples were as needs assessor, evaluator, and implementer. The examples include the following:

- A coordinated plan by the assistance community to deliver education services inside Afghanistan and in refugee villages;
- Assessment of Afghan refugee village schools in Pakistan; and
- A "Back-to-School" effort in Afghanistan after the US invasion.

Activity One: A Coordinated Plan to Deliver Primary Education

In April 1998, UNICEF-Afghanistan with SC-US and supported by the Dutch Government, convened a workshop of international and local assistance groups in Islamabad to address issues of Afghan education. The workshop entitled "Education for Afghans: Issues Confronting the Assistance Community" assembled 40 representatives of 25 Afghan and international agencies working on Afghan education. In 1996 with the Taliban ban on females in schools, a number of these agencies had suspended their education activities so as not to condone the unfair treatment of females and in hope the Taliban would relent. But by 1998 there was no sign the Taliban would rescind its ban. The international community was beginning to fear the consequences of leaving a whole generation of Afghan children without education. Most of the groups convening in Islamabad wanted to restart education services but hoped to coordinate their timing with others in the assistance community.

The participants took several days to analyze whether it was even feasible to restart education services. By the end of the workshop they had identified the opportunities and challenges to restarting their programs, and the technical and operational obstacles they would need to overcome to mount an effective program. The discussion was important because of the considerable uncertainty for some in even considering working while the Taliban were in control. The sections below summarize the points they made during the workshop.

Opportunities[19]

The participants felt the situation was not all bleak and that there were opportunities for making a new start. These included the fact that there was rising demand for schooling, including for girls, rural children, and refugees. The demand came partly from experiences in the diaspora that made many Afghans see the advantages of education. Another plus was the increased willingness of communities in Afghanistan to take responsibility for their own education services. And if the Taliban dropped the ban on girl students and female teachers there would be a whole network of government schools ready to be reinvigorated. However if the ban remained, the fluid situation in the country would probably allow programs to continue anyway despite periodic Taliban shutdowns. Most important perhaps was the renewed interest in the international community to fund Afghan education.

Challenges

The challenges anticipated by the participants were serious but not necessarily insurmountable. They included the low level of education services and infrastructure from years of conflict; the lack of government support for materials, salaries, and facilities' construction, maintenance, and repair; and the lack of government counterparts with which to work. Participants also worried about the uncertainty surrounding future directions in policy and support, and the still great potential for instability in parts of the country. And they somehow had to deal with the issue of girls' education—the still conservative views of many parents, and the bans that prevented girls from accessing opportunities or continuing beyond grade three.

Operational and Technical Issues

The participants raised a number of operational and technical problems that would need to be overcome in delivering education services inside Afghanistan and refugee villages. They defined the operational issues as unresolved policy and funding questions, and the technical issues as the lack of capacity within the assistance community to deliver services.

Operational issues that were mentioned included the assistance community's lack of well-defined goals and shared vision for the education sector in Afghanistan, and their different views on the proper role of assistance agencies in the absence of a functioning state structure. Others questioned whether even an agreed-upon approach could be brought to scale given the short-term nature of most funding, the limits on how the funds could be spent, and the difficulties of working inside the country. A major discussion surrounded the issue of whether to invest the main effort in Afghanistan or in easier-to-access Afghan refugee villages in Pakistan.

The technical issues included the assistance community's lack of expertise in the education sector, their fragmented approach, and the absence of mechanisms both to coordinate their efforts and to scale up programs. In theory the participants believed most problems could be addressed through technical means, but the difficulty was in knowing whether any assistance effort would have enough time, resources, and favorable conditions to lay a sound foundation given the uncertain future of Afghanistan.

Guidelines for Planning

The workshop participants decided that any future program should do the following:

- *Coordinate the assistance community's efforts* to deliver education cost-effectively to major segments of the population and ensure uniform quality across groups.
- *Use a principled approach* that opened up opportunities for all children regardless of their ethnic background, economic level, or sex.
- Guarantee that any *short-term investments would have long-term applicability* no matter what the future held for Afghanistan.

Developing an Options Plan

A consultant was hired to develop options for an approach that met the participants' three conditions. She reviewed the literature on Afghan education, looked at project documents of participating members' previous and current activities, and interviewed assistance staff in the field to elicit their views on what might be possible. She also visited schools in Kabul, Jalalabad, and Kunar provinces inside Afghanistan, as well as in Afghan refugee villages near Peshawar in Pakistan.

At the behest of the Afghan Coordinating Body for Afghan Relief (ACBAR)[20] in Kabul, she visited home schools and met a Taliban official in the MOE.[21]

The consultant reported her findings in three parts:

- An assessment of the assistance community's capacities;
- Staff views on renewing efforts in the education sector; and
- Options the assistance community might pursue under current conditions.

Assessment of agencies' capacities. Of the 14 assistance agencies where detailed data were gathered,[22] the consultant found that a number of them were still working inside the country in 25 of the country's 30 provinces with their heaviest concentration in areas accessible from Pakistan or Kabul, but leaving the rest of the country largely unserved or underserved. Most groups were providing formal primary programs or informal literacy courses for both boys and girls, but a few specialized in programs for girls or boys only. Many of the organizations offered training for teachers in their programs but few evaluated the impact of the training on learning. Most monitored their programs but few analyzed or reflected on their results in order to improve them. Only one group worked on curriculum development.

Interview results from the staff of participating assistance agencies. The respondents described their experiences in providing education services to Afghans and what they thought would be the issues in restarting their programs. They felt the main obstacle in urban areas would be the Taliban presence, but believed that many rural communities would be willing to provide education services if given modest support. The staff recommended taking a nonconfrontational approach with the Taliban, and urged providers to seize opportunities as they arose rather than trying to plan too much in advance. They felt the assistance community should avoid the formal government sector because of the Taliban bans on girls and women, but believed it could take a "principled approach" by supporting nonformal home and community schools. Most felt the focus should be on primary education but some felt secondary and tertiary levels shouldn't be ignored if the aim was to produce the professionals the country needed. The staff were divided on whether to focus on refugee groups where demand was high and services easier to provide, or on children inside Afghanistan where education services were needed but would be more difficult to deliver.

The staff mentioned quality issues less frequently probably because the members of these assistance agencies were mainly managers and administrators and not educators. Several admitted they lacked the expertise to address education quality and felt that even a poor quality education was better than none. Others felt quality improvements would be too costly and take too long, and would be a luxury in Afghanistan's state of emergency. The Afghan staff members, however, as parents, expressed deep concern about poor program quality and felt existing inputs, materials, and training produced inferior learning. They urged bringing program quality to international standards. Although most of the agencies approached quality through the single input of training, a few realized that the entire package of inputs needed to be improved but admitted they didn't have the skills or resources to make the changes required.

When asked how they chose textbooks for their programs, the majority said they chose them based on what teachers were accustomed to using, because of their lower cost, or simply because they were locally available in the market, but few claimed to know how to independently assess materials for their effectiveness. They said the issue of "program relevance" meant to them that all levels of education were available or, at the very least, that there were no major gaps in the curriculum such as the absence of foreign languages or meaningful discussions about topics like "peace," "the environment," or "conflict resolution."

A major weakness in the sustainability of future programs was revealed in the interviews of Afghan staff. They complained about the international community's attitude toward Afghans who should have been major players in the implementation efforts. Staff of Afghan NGOs pointed out the difficulty of building long-term capacity when their funding came mainly from low-cost, short-term contracts with international agencies. Between contracts, staff quit and it was hard to find good people when work resumed. With additional resources they could have used these slow periods to build staff capacities. They felt sidelined in the planning of projects and believed that some of the problems that arose could have been avoided if Afghans had been more involved in project designs.

Strategy recommendations. The consultant's main job was to suggest options to improve access, quality, and capacity. She therefore proposed several options to see which ones the assistance community would support. Most groups acknowledged need for reform and knew existing programs were not reaching many children who wanted them, nor did the programs enjoy the support of Afghan parents who wanted better education for their children.

The assistance groups not surprisingly disagreed about the way forward. Large donors with ongoing programs were reluctant to reorganize in order to coordinate with others, while smaller groups tended to be more receptive, feeling that improved education inputs and delivery systems would enhance their efforts. Many found it hard to visualize a program that differed from the one they had implemented earlier. Others took a wait-and-see attitude, condoning the effort but putting off the decision to join.

The comprehensive strategy that received the most international support had three main elements.

- *To improve access*: the development of a simple primary program organized around textbooks and needing little field support. These textbooks would include teacher instructions and clear steps for teaching core concepts, and as a stand alone, self-evident package could be used anywhere a literate person was willing to teach after a minimum up-front orientation.

- *To improve quality and relevance*: the establishment of basic learning standards (objectives) for primary grades and the alignment of education components—including the textbooks—to achieve them. The books would include "relevant" life skills content for the Afghan context.
- *To increase capacity*: the strengthening of the assistance community's skills—both international and Afghan—through hands-on and specialized training to develop and maintain the primary program that resulted.

This strategy put Afghans in the lead. With help from an international consultant, they would identify the basic standards for primary education, develop the new textbooks, and work out and maintain mechanisms for delivering the program. The international community would provide the organizational leadership, technical assistance, and financial support to get the program underway.

These options were presented for discussion to ACBAR, a local group set up to approve appropriate assistance activities and avoid duplication. Like the international agencies, its members at first also disagreed among themselves about the efficacy of the strategy. The lingering mistrust of foreign involvement in curriculum, the uncertainty about whether new textbooks might be another propaganda tool and other issues slowed down their approval, but eventually they supported the strategy.

What Happened Next?

Having acquired general approval from ACBAR and others in the assistance community for a program embedded in textbooks and easy to deliver, UNICEF and SC-US began organizing workshops to prepare the primary textbooks. The strategy was modeled in part on the NWFP (Pakistan) textbooks with added emphasis on making them easy to deliver with minimal support under existing conditions in Afghanistan. A benefit was that groups or individuals anywhere—in Afghanistan or in refugee villages—could adopt the textbook program voluntarily and that the organizers would not be in a position of having to choose the beneficiaries.

Preparing the program. The process of creating a transportable program in a textbook was planned as a three-step process.

- *Preparation of a set of Basic Competencies (BC)*[23] for primary math and language arts, so cooperating agencies with ongoing textbook development programs could work toward the same goals.[24]
- *Development of textbooks* geared to the basic competencies with built-in lesson plans, teacher instructions, and practical exercises. The lesson formats included everything a teacher needed to teach.
- *Editing the draft textbooks and preparing experimental editions* to be piloted in schools of participating members.

Over the next few years more than 70 Afghan educators, male and female, worked long hours under the supervision of a curriculum specialist to complete textbooks in Pashto and Dari in the core subjects of math and language arts. These subjects were seen as fundamental to all other subjects, and avoided the sensitivities surrounding topics like history, social studies, science, and religion. So as not to challenge the Taliban-approved Nebraska materials the developers called the new materials "supplementary" rather than "core" materials. That term later proved to be a mistake.

Just as the textbook drafts were finalized and ready for testing in the fall of 2001, the United States invaded Afghanistan in retaliation for al-Qaeda attacks in New York. A new Afghan Interim Government (AIG) was installed, and it seemed the opportune moment to place BC[25] materials in Afghan classrooms even though they had not undergone the testing phase. The textbooks were likely to work because of their similarities with PED textbooks that had been tested in 750 NWFP classes under reasonably similar conditions. The story continues in the third activity below that describes efforts to establish a school system for Afghanistan in the spring of 2002.

Activity Two: Assessing Refugee Village Schools in Balochistan (2000)

Meanwhile SC had concerns regarding the education services they provided to Afghan children in refugee villages in Balochistan. One was whether the Home-Based Girls' schools (HBGS) program in Balochistan was really needed, given the increasing number of formal refugee village (RV) schools being established for boys and girls. Pressure was growing to open more HBGS but SC was not sure they were needed or that existing ones provided an adequate education.

Afghan and foreign organizers of the refugee program assumed the HBGS program was inferior in quality compared with the formal refugee schools largely because HBGS and their staff did not meet the more stringent requirements of the formal RV programs. These included that school buildings exist, that teachers have academic and professional training, and that the length of the school year conform to regulations.[26] HBGS classes by contrast were located in teachers' homes, and the majority of teachers were either home-schooled by relatives or had only briefly attended formal schools and had no professional training. The school year was about the same in both kinds of school.[27] SC staff felt there might not be the same rigor of instruction in classes held in teachers' homes.

The options for girls in refugee villages included, besides HBGS, formal coed and girls-only RV schools as well as nonformal education (NFE) programs that mainly taught literacy. Parents chose options for their daughters based on the accessibility of the program, the girl's age at entry,[28] and the parent's views about girls' education, coeducation, and whether girls should be taught by male teachers.[29] In some cases parents felt the home schools provided the only acceptable alternative since they were located nearby in the all-female environment of a neighbor's home.

SC took over the management of refugee schools in Balochistan in 1995[30] and two years later established the HBGS. By 2000 there were 45 formal RV schools (6 for girls, 6 for boys and 33 mixed schools) with roughly 15,000 students, of which 33 percent were girls. The 52 one-class HBGS enrolled only about a thousand students. To open an HBGS, a literate woman applied to SC after identifying a minimum of 25 students in the 6-to-10-year age range who agreed to attend. She had to provide a dedicated room in her home where the students could meet. If her application was successful she would be given blackboard, mats, books, and other supplies, and also training in how to teach the textbooks. The books were the same German (GTZ) and/or University of Nebraska books found in formal RV schools. The teacher would take a single cohort of girls through consecutive years of schooling, usually up to and including grade three.[31] Then she might start again with a new cohort. Others wanting to study had to wait until a new HBGS class formed. The girls who started at an older age sometimes dropped out after a year or two when they reached puberty, leaving the classes with fewer students than could be cost-effectively accommodated.

Both the HBG and girls-only RV schools were supported from headquarters in Quetta by a corps of female supervisors (Field Officers or FOs) who visited them periodically to check on attendance and distribute supplies and cooking oil as an incentive to the girls and their teachers. These supervisors were key to keeping up contact with the scattered HBGS teachers and making sure the system worked.[32] Although for the most part they were active and enthusiastic about their work, the large number of schools each FO visited and their distance from headquarters made it impossible to spend much time in each one. FOs reported that their time was mainly spent on training teachers, observing classes, and distributing supplies. Most of the training occurred at the beginning of the school year to instruct teachers in the use of textbooks for the new grade that would be taught. Occasionally the FOs offered advice to teachers. They also claimed they observed teachers in the classroom and graded them on the basis of a checklist that included whether they used teachers' guides and lesson plans as directed, checked attendance and homework, knew subject matter, controlled the class, spoke politely with students, were properly dressed, and kept a clean classroom. These characteristics they assumed made a good teacher, and when asked if learning outcomes were a measure of a teacher's effectiveness, the FOs universally said no.

A Qualitative Study of HBGS

By 1999 enrollments were stagnating in the HBGS, not because girls did not want to enroll but because SC was not opening new HBG classes and because some older girls had withdrawn as they reached puberty and their parents were unwilling to let them continue. By 2000 most HBGS had only completed three grades and organizers were increasingly worried that the minimally educated teachers would not be able to cope with the more difficult subject matter of the upper primary grades. The increased demand for girls' education and the lack of new openings in HBGS was causing more parents to enroll their daughters in RV schools. The same uneven ratio of girls' enrollment compared to boys however remained constant in the villages, suggesting that places were not expanding sufficiently to meet the increasing demand for girls' schooling.

Before deciding whether to open new HBGS, SC staff wanted to be sure the quality of instruction was adequate. In May of 2000, they hired a consultant to answer some of the questions about the HBGS program. She reviewed HBGS documents, interviewed staff and supervisors, and observed HBGS classes in four out of six of the main refugee villages in Balochistan. Her findings were as follows:

- Overall the HBGS with minor exceptions[33] appeared to be doing well. Girls were attending regularly and seemed to be learning.
- The teachers and students showed a dedication and seriousness of purpose that in the consultant's view was

unmatched in her experience. Students were reading with comprehension and computed math problems to a level that seemed appropriate. Students in HBGS passed exams at roughly the same rates as children in RV schools. The exams however tested memory rather than skills so were not good measures of academic achievement.

- The HBGS class environment was pleasant and conducive to learning. Classes were small, the setting homelike and informal. Teachers adjusted the time spent on a lesson to the needs of the students rather than as in RV schools to scheduled class periods. The learning was cooperative with students helping one another and sometimes the teacher when she made mistakes.
- HBGS classes seemed to be attracting girls who would not have gone to school otherwise, because they were overage for RV schools, other programs were not accessible, or parents preferred all-female HBG classes.
- The schools offered one of the few employment opportunities for women in the villages, and that seemed to influence the girls' aspirations since many claimed they wanted to become teachers.
- The schools were virtually invisible, and so could remain open in times of turmoil in the refugee villages when formal schools had to close.
- There were weaknesses in the training of teachers, in the supervisory system, and, because of the kinds of tests used, in the ability to evaluate learning.

The few weaknesses in the program undoubtedly affected the quality of the program but it was unclear to what degree these weaknesses were any different from those in the formal RV schools.

The consultant recommended a number of actions, including the following:

- SC staff should be thinking about how HBGS could be a model for programs inside Afghanistan when refugees returned. They were low-cost and easily established in remote villages and appeared to provide a good learning environment.

- SC should be clearer about their access, quality, and equity goals. Were all girls to be given opportunities to learn or only the lucky ones admitted to the limited number of HBGS? Should as many opportunities be provided for girls as boys in refugee villages, and if so, would girls' needs be given special consideration? What standards/learning goals should the program aim for?
- Given the apparent successes of HBGS, SC should open more HBGS as soon as possible, especially where teacher-candidates had already applied and met the requirements. Demand for the schools was outstripping supply.
- Because there were difficulties finding female teachers and because of the extra costs of supervision, HBGS should continue to give priority to girls who otherwise could not access formal schools, were overage, or whose parents disapproved of them studying in RV schools.
- SC should recruit RV girl dropouts to fill vacancies in HBGS when older girls withdraw. Some of those who drop out of RV schools might be able to continue in the all-female HBGS classes in a neighbor's home.
- SC needs to work on its training, supervisory and exam systems to focus on teaching performance and learning results.

In her report the consultant suggested that training programs should go beyond just demonstrating textbooks and teacher guides and address needs observed in classrooms by trainers or specifically identified by the teachers. For example, the teachers were unaware of what learning objectives they should be teaching and how they could make sure students learned them. Better than checklists of teachers' behaviors, supervisors could administer short skill-based tests to see how effectively teachers were teaching. SC needed to develop transparent[34] skill-based tests for students to ensure they were learning basic skills as well as meeting grade-level standards that would qualify them for diplomas.

Because the consultant could not determine precisely from observations alone how the quality of teaching/learning compared in formal RV and HBGS she recommended administering standard competency tests in the two kinds of schools to make sure students were attaining appropriate primary-level skills in both.

A Quantitative Study of HBG and RV Schools

SC followed up on the recommendation that competency tests be administered to students in HBG and RV schools to determine the effectiveness of their programs. In December 2000, SC hired two consultants to undertake a "Baseline Study of Teaching-Learning in SC/US Afghan Refugee Schools of Balochistan."[35] One consultant supervised a study that measured student acquisition of core competencies in Pashto and math.[36] With help from the FO staff, competency tests were administered to 1,256 RV and HGBS students in 57 grade 3 classes[37] in 7 refugee villages.

The second consultant supervised a qualitative study of observations in language arts and math classes in thirteen formal RV and nine informal HBGS.[38] She and a Pashto-speaking staff member observed the classes and conducted interviews with teachers and students.

The main aim of the quantitative study was to compare learning results in three types[39] of refugee village schools: RV-coed, RV-girls only, and HB-girls only. The qualitative study was intended to identify possible reasons if major differences emerged in the test results of these three types of schools. SC staff as noted believed the HBGS program was inferior because of the informal learning environment and its less qualified teachers.

The Quantitative Findings

The results of the testing were highly anticipated since the topic of HBGS inferiority had been much debated. The Afghan staff in particular seemed surprised by the results. The important findings included the following:

- HBGS students consistently achieved higher learning results than students in both types of RV formal schools.

RV-coed schools came next,[40] and RV-girls' schools were significantly lower than both the other types of schools.

- Student scores were low overall (with means of 58 percent in math and 61 percent in Pashto).
- Overall, more students (30 percent) achieved an 80 percent pass rate in Pashto than in math (13 percent).
- Girls performed better in Pashto and boys performed better in math.

The findings also showed that teacher academic background and length of experience did not correlate significantly with student test results.[41] And, in terms of student learning, the checklists used by FOs to evaluate teachers did not accurately identify teachers whose students performed well on tests. The lists were better at identifying poor teachers than distinguishing average from good teachers.

The Qualitative Findings

The classroom observations and interviews suggested a number of possible reasons for the results.

- There were distinctly different learning cultures in HBG and RV schools.
- HBGS' successes may have been due to a learning environment where teachers were responsive to the needs of students, including giving them more time to master a concept if needed. HBGS teachers were more interactive with students and less likely than male teachers to lecture.
- The RV classes were more formal in nature, with greater social distance between teachers and students, and more formal arrangement of the classrooms. Teachers kept to schedules for subject lessons and used more formal ways of presenting concepts and calling on students. Children sat in assigned seats, some of which were blind areas in terms of teacher attention.
- The RV-girls only schools may have scored lowest because of factors related to the women teachers. The formal environment required them to teach more formally, by standing

at the head of the class and calling on children in some sort of order. Many commuted long distances[42] or had conflicts at home that caused them to be late or absent, and the scarcity of teachers meant there were no substitutes. The researchers found instances where teachers admitted to falsifying their own and others' attendance records.
- Student age significantly correlated with test results and HBGS students tended to be older than those in RV schools where entry ages were lower.
- The lower scores of girls in math may have been due to the fewer years of schooling of their teachers, while their better scores in Pashto may have been because teachers shortchanged math and gave more time to language arts.

School Improvement Program (SIP)

Based on the studies, the consultants prepared an outline for a school improvement program (SIP). The aim of SIP was to establish a uniformly high quality teaching-learning program for Afghan refugee children. The basis for the program would be the BC materials described in Activity One, with implementation taking place in three phases.

- *Phase One:* FOs would communicate BC learning objectives to teachers of Pashto and math so they would know what they were required to teach.[43] Assessment tests would be developed to determine whether students learned the objectives. Teachers could use their own approaches to instill these objectives during this phase but they would be held accountable for results.
- *Phase Two:* FOs would introduce BC textbooks with a brief orientation to demonstrate the lesson format. Teachers who followed the lesson formats would be presumed to produce the desired competencies. If results proved otherwise, teachers would receive more training.
- *Phase Three:* Staff members overseeing resource centers in the refugee villages along with the FOs would develop support systems for the use of BC materials, including training, testing, supervision, and feedback.

Evidence from the studies showed clearly that formal criteria for establishing schools in Afghanistan and in the refugee villages did not necessarily lead to better student learning. The studies strongly suggested that more flexibility could be exercised without compromising quality, e.g., using informal venues, teachers with lower qualifications, and more flexible classroom schedules. Furthermore, the criteria used by FOs in judging teachers could be replaced with more powerful indicators based on the results of skill tests. FOs could then focus on building the supportive structures where student learning could be improved.

Although these points were the clear implication of the studies, change is always difficult to realize and this case was no different. The consultants were not in a position to "sell" the new approach and even though the reorganization appeared simple and straightforward to them, the fixed mindset among some of the staff prevented the reform from taking place.[44]

Activity Three: Mounting a "Back-to-School" Effort for Afghan Children (2002)

The Basic Competency textbooks described in Activity One were just coming on line in the fall of 2001 as the Americans invaded Afghanistan. The plan had been to pilot them in classes of participating organizations and to continue developing elements to support their use. The main support that was contemplated was competency tests to make sure children learned the intended skills. If children demonstrated their mastery of grade-level skills, they could then be given credit. Teachers also needed a brief orientation to the new textbooks and then a more elaborated in-service training to address any difficulties they might be having and to improve their subject content knowledge and classroom management skills.

And this was not the end of needed enhancements. Writers would need to prepare further materials for higher grades to expand and enrich the content of the curriculum beyond math and language arts. The materials would need to be self-instructional for students who could read on their own but where conventional teachers might not be available for older girls or remotely located rural children in the upper grades.[45] These were issues being raised for future development of the BC materials, but events quickly overtook this discussion and eventually made most of them moot.

During the spring and summer of 2001, a staff member of an INGO had been editing the math books into a consistent format. However when the edits were complete, the Afghan authors felt the math books had been changed to such an extent that they were almost unrecognizable. Not only had a foreign staff member changed the format and the sequence of objectives the Afghans had carefully prepared, but she had substituted math problems of her own with answers she computed incorrectly! This was a huge disappointment for the UNICEF organizers who had worked out a careful process to put Afghans in charge of the content. And indeed for the Afghans it was reminiscent of the foreign community's lack of confidence in their abilities. A crisis was only averted when early drafts of the books were found and the Afghans restored the books to their original form.

This incident with the textbooks occurred just as the new Afghan Government was taking over in Kabul following the US invasion. The AIG decided to make a major push to restart schools in March 2002.[46] UNICEF was given lead responsibility to organize the Back-to-School effort, and their plan was to use the newly available BC materials. The sudden demand for the already delayed books left no time to pilot them as planned.[47]

Meanwhile, as international groups were gearing up to support the development effort in Afghanistan, UNICEF was working to put Afghans in the forefront of after-war planning. In late 2001 UNICEF sponsored a forum where Afghans from various assistance sectors prepared "vision" papers of what they hoped would come next. One of the key papers, "Framework for Afghan Education," was presented to ACBAR, the Afghan body that had approved the education options paper. ACBAR unanimously endorsed the "Framework," including the use of new BC textbooks. The "Framework" was presented in Islamabad in late November 2001 at the first major international conference on Afghanistan after the invasion,[48] and later circulated at subsequent Bonn, Berlin, Brussels, and Tokyo conferences, where it was well received and endorsed.[49] A WB/ADB/UNDP (World Bank/Asian Development Bank/United Nations Development Program) preliminary needs assessment organized in 2002 also endorsed the use of BC materials. Most of the assistance community assumed the BC books would be used in Afghan schools until the MOE had time to develop its own textbooks.

During the sessions to plan post-Taliban education, several Afghan educators complained that they had been isolated for so long from the rest of the world that they had little knowledge of how other countries addressed the kinds of education problems they would face. In response UNICEF commissioned a policy paper that was to identify common education problems, describe how other countries solved them, and suggest options that might be relevant in the Afghan context. The paper, entitled "Models, Policy Options, and Strategies: A Discussion Paper in Support of Afghan Education," was distributed to all UNICEF offices, but like the "Framework" paper its recommendations were largely ignored. For example, the paper recommended the following:

- A focus on flexible means of delivering programs rather than on school construction so programs could be implemented quickly in all locales of Afghanistan, even where buildings might not be available for some time.[50]
- Coordinating the components of the education program so they reinforced one another and aimed at achieving learning goals.
- Avoiding the old inequities in Afghan education that had focused services in urban areas. Returning to the urban bias would destroy the considerable community efforts

that had arisen as a result of Taliban neglect of the formal system.[51]

Contrary to these recommendations, donors[52] focused on school construction and distributed responsibility for program elements among various donor countries where these elements were not coordinated. Village teachers were attracted back to salaried positions in urban areas, while previous MOE employees rejoined a Ministry in Kabul that soon became top-heavy with people at headquarters.

Meanwhile as a prelude to its Back-to-School effort, UNICEF obtained permission from the Afghan Deputy Minister to publish BC materials for math and language arts, along with other textbooks that rounded out the primary curriculum, including Nebraska books devoted to religion.[53] UNICEF began printing enough textbooks for the 1.7 million children expected to enroll in schools in March 2002.[54] The consultant who had earlier developed the "options" strategy worked with the writers of the BC materials to prepare an "orientation" program for the thousands of teachers who would be using the materials for the first time. She and an assistant tried to involve officials in the MOE in the planning but officials were too occupied with politics at the time and eventually left it to the consultants to propose and implement a training plan. In effect the officials missed an opportunity to activate a large network of provincial educators who were eager to participate.

Well into the printing of the materials the Afghan Minister had a change of heart, at the urging of the US Government,[55] and declared that Nebraska books would be authorized for use in classrooms instead of the BC books, which could only be used as "supplementary materials." The Nebraska Press in Peshawar however was unable to produce the large quantity of books in time and consequently the carefully planned school opening went without these "required" materials. Despite what seemed the highly irregular nature of the Minister's late change of mind and the general consensus that the Nebraska books were of inferior pedagogical value, no one from the international community stood up for the new BC materials, and by the following year they were no longer being used in the government schools of Afghanistan.

UNICEF's Considerations in Organizing Assistance

At this stage we can look for a moment at how the main organizer of these activities, UNICEF, conceived its role in Afghan education. As a multilateral organization, UNICEF had a somewhat different mandate than a bilateral donor like USAID (see the Pakistan case for USAID's considerations). UNICEF says[56] it works through a range of local, national, and international partners to realize the educational and gender-equality goals articulated in international documents, such as the Millennium Development Goal of universal primary education and the World Declaration on Education for All. UNICEF's mandate calls for it to target children under 18 years of age and to provide support for basic education as it is locally defined. It does not normally work on formal secondary education but supports actions to ease transition into this stage, as well as providing catch up / bridging programs for out-of-school children. UNICEF does not work at the tertiary level of education except where teacher training is involved.[57]

The Afghan project fit UNICEF's mandate in a number of ways. It was responsive to the principle of access with equality and sought to build long-term Afghan capacity. The project was innovative and had the potential to provide insights that might be useful in other similar contexts of the world. It responded to the priority needs of Afghan educators and upheld UNICEF's principle of nondiscrimination.

In following its mandate UNICEF's main role is usually to coordinate and provide leadership on children's issues. It does not have the capacity (staff/teams) to implement projects directly. Although governments are its main partners, it also works through a variety of organizations that are registered with the local governments where it works. In an emergency it may take a more hands-on role.

In the Afghan project, UNICEF and Save the Children assumed complementary roles, while at the same time together providing intellectual and technical leadership. UNICEF took the convening role and provided a platform for advocacy of Afghan education. As an intergovernmental organization its neutral umbrella allowed NGOs and Afghan educators to come together and work on their common priorities. Save the Children on the other hand was able to take on staff and consultants to work on the specialized activities the project required. UNICEF's neutral umbrella also meant that the products of the activities—in this case, textbooks—had a better chance of being accepted by various political actors in Afghanistan than if they had been produced solely by a bilateral donor.[58]

In terms of where and with whom it can work, UNICEF is bound by the decisions of its Executive Board and its Global Mandate and not necessarily by the preferences of specific donors if they should differ.[59] In certain cases UNICEF negotiates with nonstate actors if they have control over children, but in all instances UNICEF staff must adhere to its humanitarian principles. In the Afghan situation UNICEF and other UN agencies negotiated with the Taliban to try and persuade them to give women and girls rights to education and employment but with limited success. During much of the period in which the project activities took place the Taliban constituted the de facto authority in Afghanistan, even though the international community did not treat them as a recognized government entity. This complicated the situation for UNICEF and other members of the assistance community, forcing them to use creative "work around" modalities as they termed them. The problems would likely have increased if the BC books had been disseminated under a Taliban regime. The plan as noted had been to supply them first through other organizations for use in their programs. But in supplying these organizations with money and support and leaving them to negotiate their own activities with the Taliban, UNICEF might have been accused of the morally indefensible act of transferring risk to other organizations. In this and similar circumstances UNICEF should not violate its own requirement that it take "a principled approach" or at a minimum "do no harm."

LESSONS FROM AFGHANISTAN

Difficulties of Coordination

These efforts in Afghan education show the difficulties of coordinating the actions of multiple donors and organizations. Each agency in this instance had its own mission and often feared the loss of visibility if its contribution was merged with those of others. It proved difficult, for example, for bilateral donors already invested in the sector to abandon their activities or admit that their efforts could be supplanted by something better. It required an act of faith to support a program that only promised to be more cost-effective and efficient in the future. Several groups understandably continued to use their own instructional materials, teaching approaches, and evaluation methods during development of the new books.

In order to provide a coordinating mechanism for the various groups who might use it, the project created a single set of learning objectives (basic competencies) to give a uniform framework for developing materials, training, and measuring achievement. But although one main donor used the framework to produce new materials, others did not. A consequence of the fact that few agencies fully invested in the project was that when the Minister replaced the BC books, none was willing to risk criticizing his actions.[60] They tried to continue operating as before, until they discovered that the Nebraska books had been mandated by the Minister for all the programs in Afghanistan.[61]

Difficulty in Introducing New Ideas

A parallel problem emerging in this case was the difficulty of winning acceptance of ideas even when the evidence was overwhelmingly in their favor. Focusing on flexible delivery, for example, was and is perhaps the only way to bring education services to remote areas of Afghanistan. And yet this idea was not readily adopted by foreigners or Afghans alike in the aftermath of the US invasion. They rushed instead to achieve an "ideal" system of well-constructed buildings and highly qualified teachers in an effort to mirror states with well-resourced, long-established programs and an abundance of well-qualified personnel. Afghanistan's state of emergency unfortunately did not allow for this kind of luxury and as a consequence resources were squandered on high-cost items like construction that made it impossible to reach many children needing a program.

Again and again ideas were placed on the table with supporting arguments and yet they had difficulty winning acceptance. There were the strategy options for a coordinated effort to address Afghan education that struggled for the approval of the assistance community as well as ACBAR. There were recommendations for a school improvement plan coming out of the studies of refugee schools that were resisted. There was the Afghan "vision" framework and the UNICEF policy paper suggesting ideas for post-Taliban education that were ignored by postwar planners. Finally there were the BC materials specifically designed for the conditions of Afghanistan that were set aside in favor of a program widely considered to be inferior. In these examples we see the powerful impact of authorities with entrenched preconceptions that cause them to ignore any evidence that contradicts their beliefs. Part of the problem in both Afghanistan and Pakistan is a genuine distrust of research that people believe—probably rightly in many cases—has been manipulated to support their authors' point of view.

The reverse of course was also true in Afghanistan; that bad ideas often seem to have a life of their own despite overwhelming evidence against them—for example, the Afghans' continuing resistance to nonformal approaches to education, a steadfast belief in the characteristics that make good teachers, confidence in rote forms of instruction, and many others. No amount of evidence easily shakes confidence in these beliefs.

Part of the problem is of course that reforms sometimes take their inspiration from outdated or inappropriate models (e.g., Nebraska textbooks), donor fads (e.g., active learning pedagogies), or the shifting time-bound priorities of donors (e.g., the focus on girls' education, child trafficking, a focus on youth, or on gender mainstreaming). Education reform is a long-term process that only succeeds when local authorities believe in the ideas and muster the political will to stay the course beyond the end of the assistance period.

Afghan Capacity and Staff Roles

On a positive note, the Afghan developers of the BC textbooks proved to be a dedicated group of educators who quickly mastered the skills to prepare systematic learning materials. They were helped by an experienced curriculum specialist who demanded a high level of professionalism in their work (for which she was the judge) but who also understood the need for Afghans to be in charge of the textbook content designed for their own children. The final element was a capable UN project officer who shepherded the activities to a successful conclusion by stressing Afghan participation and deflecting objections of donors who worried about competition with their own contributions. She accepted the fact that not every group could commit to the strategy.[62] This project was one of those happy collaborations when the main people involved in implementing it were of similar mind and worked enthusiastically toward the same goal.

The Political Issue

A main lesson from the Afghan case (as we saw also in Egypt and Pakistan) was the overriding importance of politics: both the needs and priorities of donor governments and local authorities. In Afghanistan the hiatus in the provision of education services during the 1990s left few experienced

Afghan government authorities in 2002 willing to support reform. Those brought in from the Afghan diaspora to assume leadership jobs were similarly inexperienced in the sector and often had other agendas. This particular situation raises the question of whether efforts such as these organized under UNICEF and initiated outside the country (in Pakistan) even with a strong involvement of Afghans could ever have been accepted and sustained under conditions like these where a new government wanted to show its own authority. Among other problems, the timing simply wasn't right to introduce a new program no matter how promising it might have been.

On the donor side, the United States sought a visible role in the education sector by funding construction, textbooks, and training. As is true of all major donors, the United States operates within constraints imposed by legislation (e.g., "Buy America") and other national political considerations. In this period of assistance a large share of US funds to Afghanistan was spent on foreign consultants' salaries, US commodities, and in the case of Nebraska, US-developed materials. At its peak roughly 80 percent of US assistance for Afghanistan in the early years was spent outside the country, mostly in the United States. After Afghans objected more funds began to flow into their economy. The point that should be taken from the collapse of the BC project is that where highly visible reform activities with multiple actors and multiple agendas exist, conditions are ripe for political as opposed to development interests to prevail. It is one of the reasons that embedding reform routines in a quiet way into bureaucracies is often a better guarantee of long-term survival than touting results in a highly visible way where they are vulnerable to political priorities.

When assistance efforts do not achieve their intended results for whatever reason as happened when programs were abruptly stopped in Pakistan and Afghanistan, local people become cynical about the process and are less willing to cooperate the next time around.[63] One might conclude from these cases that development efforts at the local level, through local agencies and local people, although perhaps not as well funded, may have a better chance of succeeding over the long run. Local efforts, on the other hand, rarely achieve the scale or variety of beneficiaries that assistance support to national programs can reach.

In the "Conclusions and Commentary" chapter that follows we will look further at some of the lessons from these cases.

Chapter 6

Conclusions and Commentary

We need to inspire people not intimidate them. There's something about all aid that is subversive.

Paul Theroux

Introduction

These case studies will hopefully begin to fill the important gap in the literature on foreign assistance—the lack of materials describing the field practice of development. The three parts of the book seek to simulate the understandings practitioners acquire during their professional careers: the knowledge of issues, background in how others deal with similar problems, and an understanding of what it's like to implement projects and confront obstacles in the field. This conclusion chapter suggests some of the insights a practitioner might draw from these cases.

The book also indirectly addresses larger questions of international development. For years there have been complaints that foreign assistance is not as effective as it should be. The cases in this book suggest that the problem, at least here, was not so much a lack of effort or even of poorly designed solutions, as it was the competing political and development interests affecting reforms. Looking back, it is painful to think what might have been different if political interests had not interfered in Pakistan and Afghanistan to shut down the projects prematurely.

Some would argue that the cases represent an old way of doing "development"—where outside consultants determine what and how reforms should be implemented. Even if true, it's important to assess what went right or wrong in these approaches in order to move toward more effective ways of "doing development." As long as policy makers and donors are willing to invest in reforms there is still time to shape the agenda.

Case Similarities and Differences

The book presents a small number of cases in order to be able to describe the implementation process in detail. Their similarities in many ways exceeded their differences and they therefore provide more limited insights than might have occurred if education assistance were described in more disparate parts of the world. Some of the similarities included the following:

- All three countries had *Muslim majorities* with long experience of Koranic education. Islam in general encourages education and the Koran in particular urges Muslims to seek knowledge. However the Islamic method of transmitting knowledge inspired a model for teaching and learning that still persists in many of the regions' public schools. Based on rote learning and respect for authoritative sources, the model discourages critical thinking and problem-solving skills that educators feel children need in the modern world.
- All had *similar challenges*—how to get more children into school; how to achieve the country's academic goals; and how to strengthen local capacities to deliver education services. These challenges, in differing degree, stemmed from similar conditions—family poverty, traditional views, insufficient resources, and poorly performing bureaucracies.

- All three projects were fortunate enough to *have adequate funding*, in Egypt and Pakistan because the US Government wanted to show political support for these countries, and in Afghanistan because the UN considered education services essential and made their efforts modest but potentially with broad impact.
- All the projects had *large construction components* to expand schooling opportunities for rural children, especially girls. In Egypt construction was spurred by the need to spend large sums of mandated assistance quickly and in Pakistan and Afghanistan (in the post-Taliban era) to provide visible evidence of assistance support. Although local communities are understandably interested in construction projects, this approach is not the most effective way to spread education opportunities widely, since buildings have little direct influence on learning, which can take place in any secure, quiet place. The focus on construction diverts resources and attention from other more important education goals.
- All of the countries had bureaucracies that *set formal requirements*—technical specifications for buildings and rigid qualifications for teachers—before a formal program would be provided. This rigidity discouraged nonformal initiatives and limited delivery to hard-to-reach children.
- All three countries *failed to adequately address the specific reasons children remained out of school*, even though the reasons and locations of these children were well-known.

Similar conditions can be found in other parts of the developing world, but it is still important to use caution in applying these lessons to other areas without ensuring first through limited trials that they work.

There were also important differences among the cases that affected reforms.

- *Different eras.* They took place in different decades—Egypt in the 1980s, Pakistan in the late 1980s and early1990s, and Afghanistan in the late 1990s and early 2000s—and thus each subsequent project benefitted to some extent from lessons learned in earlier projects.

- *Different donor/organizer modalities.* The main initiators—USAID and UNICEF—played different roles. USAID funded reforms and contracted experts through consulting companies to shape and implement activities. This meant in Egypt and Pakistan that companies added an additional layer of authority and accountability that, for the consultants, was mostly mediated through a Chief of Party (COP) in the field. The consulting company in turn reported to and resolved issues with the donor.[1] UNICEF on the other hand acted as convener for the main players to discuss education concerns in Afghanistan and the education officer worked with the consultant to gain local approval for proposed options, and partnered with an INGO that could sponsor workshops and hire consultants. A UNICEF staff member often accompanied the consultant on trips to the field and remained actively involved in ensuring activities moved forward.
- *Different approaches to education problems.* The donors and developers approached reform in different ways. In Egypt they focused on construction and practical courses, in Pakistan on a comprehensive system-wide approach, and in Afghanistan a "package" program that could be easily delivered.[2]
- *Different local conditions.* The countries also had different geographies and unique historical experiences with education that affected how they perceived the needs of their systems and their own roles in reform. Most populations in Egypt are easily reached along the Nile, whereas Pakistan and Afghanistan have terrains that include high mountain ranges and remote difficult-to-access villages. Historically Egypt experienced an education introduced by outsiders, which led to improved social status for graduates. The area that is now Pakistan was largely neglected by British occupiers and focused therefore on religious learning. Afghanistan coped with a Soviet occupation that used education largely as a political tool.

The Impact of Assistance in the Three Cases

Even though the reforms showed promise, the results in all three cases fell short of original expectations. The main reasons were poorly conceived details in planning, unexpected obstacles in the local context, and external political decisions.

- In Egypt a focus on enrollments without improvements in the academic program led to deteriorating learning outcomes. The practical courses that were meant to make schooling more relevant failed to fit the local context.
- In Pakistan, the abrupt cessation of donor support after four rather than the planned ten years of implementation left few traces of the reform activities.
- In Afghanistan the unexpected American takeover of the country and strong international competition to support the new government meant the newly completed Afghan program fell victim to competing political interests.

Optimists would say that no effort is entirely wasted—that the experience of participating in a development process continues to exert an influence on those who were involved. While this may be true for individual participants, their newly found skills are unlikely to find expression if local conditions discourage their use. It is not clear what remains of the carefully honed skills of educators in Pakistan and Afghanistan, or more to the point whether these skills can be put into practice.

Constraints

If potential solutions are not difficult to identify, as the cases suggest, why are there so many failures in education assistance? Project proposals submitted by contractors commonly balance the elements conducive to reform (opportunities) against those that obstruct reform (constraints).

Before listing the constraints, which were numerous, it is useful to review the opportunities that were present at the start of these projects. The opportunities included (with the exception of Afghanistan under the Taliban) the existence of institutional structures charged with responsibility for the education sector, a cadre of seemingly enthusiastic officials wanting reforms, and an international community willing to support them.

Against these opportunities, a number of constraints surfaced to prevent the full attainment of the objectives. While some constraints were amenable to change, others proved virtually impossible to overcome. Some of the most important constraints are described below.

Conflicting Views of Development

Interpersonal relations at all levels significantly affected reforms. This issue is rarely discussed in the literature probably because it varies so much in different contexts and is difficult to address. It becomes especially important in field operations where people work together on a daily basis. Conflicts were particularly visible in Pakistan where, in just one example, district education officers resisted becoming managers of reform as envisioned by foreign consultants when the new role didn't square with their image of themselves as distributors of patronage.

Also clear from the Pakistan example were differences among foreign consultants in how they perceived their roles—as advisors "waiting to be asked" or reformers actively pursuing changes. In the Afghan case, a conflict arose when a foreigner made changes in new textbooks, demonstrating her lack of confidence in the Afghans' ability to write good instructional materials. In other respects the Afghan case in its initial stages proceeded smoothly because Afghans chose and developed the interventions themselves while foreigners mainly provided technical and financial support. Problems arose only after the US invasion when textbooks became an international political issue.

Cultural Differences[3]

Culture had a strong influence on the views of participants in all three cases. The Western participants tended to focus on learning outcomes and results while local officials worried more about how reforms affected themselves and their personal networks—their seniority and authority positions, and the benefits that might accrue from being involved in the assistance efforts. These differences emanated from, on the one hand, outsiders who believed strongly that every child had a right to a quality education and that services should be provided in an impersonal way, and on the other hand, members of communally based societies who felt strong obligations to tribal, familial, and other groups, and sometimes saw reforms as restricting their abilities to fulfill these obligations. These contrasting perspectives affected how participants viewed such issues as where education should take place, what kinds of qualifications were needed to become teachers and students, and how education should be conducted—its approaches, methods, content, training, and spoken and unspoken goals.[4] These differing perspectives also affected how the two sides looked at foreign assistance and the motivations of both donors and recipients. Outsiders unwittingly disrupted personal relationships in just about everything they did, including the kinds of reforms they encouraged.[5]

Outsider Influences

There were two major ways outsiders affected the shape of reform. The first was through the strings donors attached to assistance that in some instances seemed to promote their own interests more than those of the beneficiaries. The donors limited the issues that could be addressed, some of the actions that could be taken, affected the design of projects, and established benchmarks local communities needed to meet. Congressional directives to USAID, for example, often specified the amounts of support, the mechanisms, the time frames, and the results that were to be expected. USAID then translated these parameters into project requirements stipulating the activities and staffing needed to accomplish the goals. With pressure to show results, USAID often insisted on herculean efforts in tight and unrealistic time frames, and during early stages of projects when they had more leverage, insisted upon changes in local policies and procedures to ease the process of reform. In Pakistan, for example, USAID encouraged the Pakistanis to separate the primary department from the rest of preuniversity education. Once projects were under way—when donors no longer had the same leverage—it was more difficult to make needed structural changes or penalize local governments when they didn't fulfill their agreements. The Egyptian bureaucracy for example failed to meet their agreements to maintain newly constructed USAID schools or provide raw materials for the practical courses, and Pakistani officials often failed to meet agreed-upon annual milestones. In both instances, USAID did not impose penalties or insist that local authorities uphold their agreements, thereby almost guaranteeing that future efforts would be further compromised or the achievement of results slowed.

Outside consultants—no matter how well-meaning—often sent contradictory messages to their local counterparts by implying their solutions would work even before testing them in the local context. When they failed to solve local problems, people lost faith in the consultants' expertise and turned to more enduring "visible solutions" like buildings. Visiting trainers for example left little impact on teaching/learning when they stressed child-centered approaches that were difficult to implement in large classes with different local expectations for teacher-pupil relations. In all three country cases, outsider assistance failed to find lasting ways to improve the academic program: in Egypt because they largely ignored quality issues, in Pakistan because support was withdrawn early, and in Afghanistan because the full program was never implemented. These failures were not so much a matter of bad ideas as they were a consequence of poor decisions. But they proved to have a long-term impact on the education system and, equally important, on local willingness to accept outsiders' ideas in the future.

In theory, if not always in real life, outsiders can play a helpful role. Their broader expertise and experience gives them a tool chest of potential solutions that local officials may not be aware of. They can mediate between donor intentions and local expectations, as for example in the design phase of the Pakistan program when consultants could clarify donor intentions to local officials and relay back local officials' expectations for the program. Backed by resources, consultants can also push for changes that insiders entrenched in their underfunded bureaucracies might not even imagine. In the best instances, outsiders can offer appropriate options and use their influence to implement those chosen by local officials. In the worst, they are insensitive to how existing systems serve their counterparts' interests and fail to alleviate the negative consequences of their project activities.

Insider Influences

Local officials in these cases can claim their own share of blame for stalling reforms. Often they lacked the political will or the economic incentives to address fundamental obstacles. In Egypt one such obstacle was and continues to be "private tutoring," which encourages poor teaching during school hours and raises education costs for parents. In Pakistan, problems of corruption and weak management are endemic; and in Afghanistan corruption and insecurity disrupt participation and learning. No matter how difficult these constraints are to resolve, there is little hope of developing effective education programs as long as they persist or at least are not addressed.

As recipients of assistance, local beneficiaries have their own issues to resolve. They have to ask themselves to what extent they are willing to make the difficult changes in policies and institutions to obtain foreign resources. Do the requirements of foreign project design put an unsustainable burden on their ability to continue the reforms in the future?

What about dependency—is foreign assistance a new form of colonialism, as some argue, that keeps local politicians from making the hard decisions that are needed to solve their countries' long-standing problems? In all three countries, tax structures are weak or virtually nonexistent and donor support means local officials can ignore or postpone important decisions about how to pay for the country's development.

In the end the insider role is of course indispensible. In the best instances, insiders offer advice about solutions, and warn against inappropriate ones—whether for fiscal or human capacity reasons, or because they are incompatible with local customs and cultures. In the worst instances insiders fail to engage for whatever reasons and let projects flounder in ways that could have been avoided.

One observer[6] noted that the theme that emerges repeatedly in discussions with beneficiaries in various countries is the demeaning ways that both material aid and technical assistance are provided. Disrespect is conveyed in language, in processes, in attitudes—sometimes explicitly and far more often implicitly. It is this kind of relationship that needs to change.

Other Factors Slowing Reform

One of the more persistent and difficult obstacles in these cases was the uncritical bureaucratic belief in the forms rather than the functions of education systems. Consider for example the redundancies in data collection in Pakistan because different authorities ask for them, the lack of coherence between parts of the education system in Afghanistan, the disabling civil service rules in Pakistan that can't be changed, and the persistent belief that exams are meant to eliminate academically weak children from school rather than identify areas where they might learn more. In Pakistan, the education units involved in creating exams, curriculum, and training programs resisted becoming involved on the reform process, and consequently played a major role in perpetuating the rote learning methods educators were trying to change. Pakistanis also saw little need to measure success. They accepted as measures of quality such proxies as literacy figures,[7] teacher-student ratios, class size, lists of teacher characteristics, and the availability of instructional materials, libraries, and other amenities. Only near the end of the assistance efforts were more reliable measures being established but these were lost as was most everything else when the program ceased.

In all three countries, officials essentially ignored research results that consultants believed should substantiate the need for certain kinds of reforms. Even with ample evidence that teacher training programs in Pakistan had no perceptible impact on student learning,[8] training institutes refused to change their curriculum. The training programs had little impact for several reasons, including that training was not tied to learning objectives, that it focused on methods and ignored weak teacher content knowledge, and that it tended to be based on outmoded or inappropriate foreign models that didn't fit the local context. Even though minor inroads were made through donor-supported activities, training remained an obstacle to improving learning.

Consequences of Continuing the Status Quo

There are serious consequences for current and future generations if the status quo in the education sector continues in these countries. Some are obvious——in particular the continuing lack of schooling opportunities for hard-to-reach populations and the long-term impact of poor academic programs on the countries' prosperity as well as its security. Others may not be so obvious such as the connection between poor quality programs and the continued low rates of participation, especially for girls. Addressing only quantity or quality issues in isolation is not the answer to any of the sector's problems since they so intimately affect one another.

As long as there is no effort to hold educators accountable for poor learning results, program quality is not likely to improve no matter what kinds of reforms are implemented. If system administrators are unwilling or unable to hold themselves and others accountable for education attainment or can't think flexibly about delivering and crediting academic programs, then certain children will forever be denied the benefits of a quality education. If bureaucracies fail to identify and resolve problems, programs will continue to produce graduates that are ill-equipped for the modern world.

Summary Lessons

Seeking a New Approach

The "old way" of doing development where outsiders survey the situation, make recommendations, and actively organize reforms is outmoded for a number of reasons. In addition to all the valid reasons for local ownership identified in the Paris Declaration,[9] it is simply the case that consultants' fees are too expensive to keep them in the field for long using up a large share of the assistance funds. Security situations are often too unstable for foreigners to move freely in these countries as they once did and local communities have been disappointed too many times to feel the same enthusiasm for foreign-run projects. An important additional reason for reform to stay in local hands is that many local educators now are sophisticated about what works in their own countries, and understand, better than outsiders, how to adapt the experiences of other countries to their own needs.

One would be naïve however to think that leaving donor-supported development entirely in the hands of local communities solves all problems. In fact it raises issues that may be even harder to resolve. Even reform-minded insiders have difficulty confronting vested interests in their own bureaucracies, and many lack the skills donors require for transparency and accountability. In this respect outsiders with resources still possess leverage that even the most qualified insiders may lack. Almost certainly new systems and more reliable measures need to be developed to ensure that resources are spent transparently and well.

Recommending a Model

The case examples describe the way assistance was carried out in three specific countries. As already noted, caution needs to be exercised when applying these examples to other situations. However the cases do suggest a generic "process model" that might be reasonably applied where the goal is to ensure that as many children as possible acquire basic academic skills. Taking a process approach doesn't guarantee a solution to all education problems, but if carried out carefully, it promises that more children will achieve more of the desired learning outcomes. This model that is as suited to developed countries as to developing countries is so self-evident that one wonders why it isn't applied more often. Not only is it likely to produce better results but it can be shaped to achieve them in locally appropriate ways that are fundamental to the goals of education.[10]

The key steps include the following:

- *To achieve universal education (quantity),* focus on flexible delivery to out-of- school children, shaping delivery to the special circumstances of children so that they find it easy to attend. What that means is finding convenient venues (of any kind), literate persons to teach, providing self-evident instructional materials, keeping the costs for parents low, and making sure children obtain certificates when they demonstrate mastery of predetermined skill levels. It *does not* mean costly buildings or insistence on formal academic or professional criteria for teachers. It *does* mean that to reach out-of-school children and keep them in school as long as possible, governments need to "lighten up" on formal requirements and shape delivery to children's needs, recognizing that the current "one formula fits all" model is limiting participation.
- *To provide effective academic programs (quality),* focus programs on learning objectives as these are defined by the country itself. Ensure by measuring results that each element in the instructional system contributes to and reinforces the others in improving learning outcomes. For the core subjects of math and language arts, the standard competencies are well-known and can be assessed by breaking

down the skills needed to read, write, comprehend, and solve math problems and testing them. Other subjects such as history and social studies depend on these basic competencies but their content can be tailored individually to the needs of a country. Achieving a quality program *does not* imply relying only on certain kinds of teaching methods or training. It *does* mean setting clear learning goals and ensuring that methods, training, and instructional content all work to achieve those goals. It also means developing detailed measures linked to learning objectives.

- *To manage schooling programs effectively,* focus management on producing learning results, identifying and maintaining program successes, and identifying and addressing weaknesses, setting up a process for the continuous improvement of learning, and demanding accountability from those responsible for producing results. The best management training is hands-on where managers identify the problems and potential solutions—with technical help as needed—and work to implement them using clear measures that ensure relevant impact. Managers need to assess project results with both formative and summative evaluations, the former to track progress during the project so changes can be made before it's too late, and the latter to make sure final results meet the intended goals. Evaluations provide information on why programs succeed or fail and are needed to suggest how they might work even better next time.

By keeping the focus on specific learning objectives, much waste and superfluous investment can be avoided. Most countries already have the institutional structures in place to manage the sector, to create and deliver inputs, and to administer schooling programs, and therefore, in theory at least, it should not require major investment to improve their performance.

A Combined Outcomes/People Approach

Critics may complain that a process model appeals more to Westerners, since it calls for tweaking inputs until they produce better results, rather than accommodating the people-based approaches more common in some developing countries. The model however can actually serve as a meeting point for the two points of view. Once the goals (products) are defined,[11] solutions can be people-driven as, for example, when schooling venues are shaped to the needs of different beneficiaries, when locally defined learning objectives are taught in a way that is locally appropriate, and when local managers control the process and tools that make reforms happen. The main point is to build systematically on models that have worked in the past and avoid models that haven't. Most people would agree that learning is the goal, and that the specifics of the approach are not as important as making sure the learning is achieved.[12]

Cost-Effective Ways to Effect Change

Increasingly donors look for inexpensive ways to effect large-scale change. Comprehensive projects like the one in Pakistan that addressed problems across the education sector are probably a thing of the past. The case studies suggest however that there may be simple, inexpensive ways to drive change. The four cost-effective actions below, for example, could make a significant impact in moving education systems in the right direction.

- Encouraging MOEs to have well-defined and detailed *learning objectives* by subject and grade to serve as the basis for a quality academic program.
- Developing *skill-based exams* based on these objectives and letting teachers know which items will be tested. Teaching to exams is an asset in this case.
- Developing mechanisms that can *flexibly deliver programs to children in different contexts* by, for example, adapting textbooks (through teacher guides or embedding instructions and exercises in the books) so they incorporate in a single package everything a literate person needs to teach.
- Using the country's learning objectives as a basis for *equivalency credit* so children studying in any environment can be rewarded once they demonstrate these skills on tests.

These four actions—defining the goals, developing appropriate measures, facilitating delivery, and rewarding attainment—are a start in creating an effective schooling program. They can be achieved within existing structures, and with minimum investment and technical support. In fact they could be implemented by determined local educators with little or no support from outsiders.

Incentives and Disincentives

The cases show that an important ingredient of success is in holding officials and staff accountable for learning results. One way is through targeted incentives/disincentives that encourage people to make desired changes in behavior. This may be as simple as making effective behaviors easier to follow than to ignore, as in Pakistan where teachers found it easier to follow the new lesson format than to continue their old practices. Another was to install procedures such as periodic testing that helped teachers to gauge their successes. An effective incentive was the posting of teacher-candidates' scores on subject knowledge exams to goad principals of training institutes into correcting problems in their training. Although incentives work much of the time, sometimes they fail and need remedial support such as focused training to correct poor results. With effective indicators and careful monitoring, the problem becomes manageable since the measures show exactly where and what support is needed.

USAID's Reformulated Approach

A New Approach

In 2010 after much discussion, USAID reformulated its assistance policies. USAID officials explained that a Quadrennial Diplomacy and Development Review (QDDR) would be conducted four times a year to make sure the new policies were on course and effective. The new approach overall would stress the importance of seeing that diplomacy and development would be mutually reinforcing, and that civilians would carry out development activities by involving diverse sectors of the local population including nonstate actors in "partnerships not patronage." The United States would engage in strategic dialogue with emerging powers, enhance regional capacities, and reform and deliver results through multilateral organizations (presumably such groups as the UN and regional organizations). The United States would consolidate functional areas into ones where it had a comparative advantage: sustainable economic growth, democracy and governance, food security, global health, climate change, and humanitarian assistance. The consolidation would mean that the United States could apply its resources with a depth and scale that would make sustainable change possible. Women and girls would remain a priority and their concerns would be integrated into all development programs.

To do all this, USAID would triple its staff and improve its leadership capacity to enable it to coordinate all assistance efforts of US agencies operating abroad. It would draw on the skills of these agencies before turning to outside contractors. It would leverage technology whenever possible to achieve results. USAID would also measure outputs (results) not inputs (although that is essentially what is being measured—the extent to which inputs increase results), and would stress transparency and sustained commitment.

The concerns expressed in the QDDR seem to stem from experiences in Afghanistan and Iraq when the US military took on many of the nation-building activities in the aftermath of the wars there. The new approach would put assistance back into civilian hands under the auspices of USAID and supervised by the State Department. From a field practitioner's point of view this makes it more, rather than less, likely that assistance would be subjected to political interests rather than development needs. On the other hand one can see that this new approach removes some of the layers of accountability and authority—the consulting companies and even consultants in some cases—and the excessive burdens of high overheads and some salary costs.

According to USAID officials, the new approach does not downplay education, especially where girls are concerned, but aid to basic education was in fact cut by $185 million or 17 percent and the USAID Director at the time admitted he would "not be able to protect non-Pakistan and non-Afghan girls' education." The new "business model for education" involves "strengthening systems of education abroad as opposed to training teachers ourselves." USAID would be looking to achieve clear goals in "reducing illiteracy by a certain percentage" and tying them to the areas of highest concerns to USAID: economic growth, democracy and governance, and better health and food security.

From a field perspective, actions speak louder than expressed intentions, so we will have to see whether this approach produces better results than previous ones. Certainly without better measures of results than we have now it would be difficult to know whether the efforts are succeeding in the education sector.

The Big Question

Field practitioners are often so immersed in day-to-day implementation that they spend little time considering the broader questions of international assistance. The main one is whether foreign assistance is the answer to the kinds of problems we are trying to solve. The cautious reply is that sometimes it helps and sometimes it doesn't. Increasingly, however, observers—usually local people, dismayed at what they see in their own countries—are suggesting that foreign assistance may be more of a detriment than a help, except of course where crises require humanitarian aid. One writer[13] whose thesis is typical of this perspective, calls for a halt in aid for Africa and makes the point already noted briefly that aid money lets countries avoid the hard decisions that might put their nations on a more solid economic track. She stresses the free-market model because as she says, "no economic ideology other than the one rooted in the movement of capital and competition has succeeded in getting the greatest numbers of people out of poverty, in the fastest time."[14] She cites the examples of South Africa and Botswana that withdrew voluntarily from the "aid-based development model." A particularly interesting point she makes is that the ever-forgiving "open purse of aid" permits high officials to make personal shopping trips every year, while if they had to finance these trips from the private cash of a free-market model they would "only get away with it once."[15] Such critiques have a point and are worth considering.

FINAL WORD

Development is a human activity and is thus subject to the messiness of human behavior. At present much donor assistance relies on conventional approaches that are piecemeal and unfocused—a training here, a workshop there. A major problem is the current divide between those organizations that formulate policy (even with local input) on a grand scale and those who test ideas on the ground. Even while those formulating policies are responding to their constituencies and funding pressures, they also need to check the practicality of their ideas on the ground. Practitioners usually know where the delivery gaps are, what needs to change, and what the local capabilities are to effect reforms on the ground. They also know that the grand designs of policy makers are often too grand to implement effectively in the field. The bottom line is that both policy makers and practitioners need to strive for a clearer vision, achievable goals, and, above all, simplicity. Development work may be messy but it is possible to make solid improvements over time with these caveats.

NOTES

CHAPTER 1

1. Timothy Morris. 1991. *The Despairing Developer: Diary of an Aid Worker in the Middle East.* London and New York: I. B. Taurus.
2. Ibid., p. 1.
3. Robert Klitgaard. 1990. *Tropical Gangsters: One Man's Experience with Development and Decadence in Deepest Africa.* New York: Basic Books.
4. Ibid., x.
5. The evolutionary approach was espoused by the anthropologist Leslie White.
6. These are a type of project often promoted by the US Government in places like Afghanistan where they are hoping to show results in a short time frame.
7. Communally based societies with a strong Muslim majority may sign international human rights declarations but often add the condition that the principles only hold as long as they don't conflict with Islam. It is the author's view that at least part of the unease comes from wanting to balance people's duties with their rights, in other words they are uncomfortable when obligations are ignored.
8. Tamim Ansary. 2009. *Destiny Disrupted: A History of the World through Islamic Eyes.* New York: Public Affairs.
9. Ibid., p. 353.
10. Haim Malka and Jon B. Alterman. 2006. *Arab Reform and Foreign Aid: Lessons from Morocco.* Washington, D.C.: Center for Strategic and International Studies.
11. Ibid., pp. 61–62.
12. We have one of the lowest ratios of foreign assistance of all the developed countries at around 1 percent of GNP.
13. This compares with, for example, democracy promotion, civil society development, and economic and legal reforms, all areas with greater sensitivity surrounding them.

14. UNESCO. 2010. Reaching the Marginalized: EFA Monitoring Report. Oxford, UK: Oxford Press.
15. Basic education is defined differently in different countries but usually includes grades one through eight or nine.
16. Deon Filmer. 1999. "Educational Attainment and Enrollment Profiles: A Resource Book Based on Analysis of Demographic and Health Survey Data," www.worldbank.org/research/projects/edattain/edattain.htm. Accessed in April 2011.
17. Barbara Herz and Gene B. Sperling. 2004. *What Works in Girls' Education: Evidence and Policies from the Developing World*. New York: Council on Foreign Affairs, p. 21 ff.
18. The World Economic Forum's Gender Gap Index. 2011. As reported in *Newsweek*, March 14, 2011, p. 50.

Chapter 2

1. Most of the projects are either completed or have been established for some time. The reason for using these older projects is that reports of their effectiveness if they exist at all take time to appear.
2. Nader Fergany, Ilham Farmaz, and Christiane Wissa. 1997. "Enrollment in Primary Education and Cognitive Achievement in Egypt, Changes and Determinants." In *Determinants of Educational Achievement and Attainment in Africa: Findings from Nine Case Studies,* ed. Ronald G. Ridker. Washington, D.C.: USAID Africa Bureau.
3. These figures appear to contradict later figures in the Egypt case study, but in fact they may be compatible because during this period population growth rates were increasing at rates faster than schooling opportunities were being provided and enrollments claimed for USAID-built school areas were higher than rates shown for non-USAID sites.
4. Some criticized this policy saying it should have arranged for both to continue their education.
5. Anil B. Deolalikar. 1997. "Increasing School Quantity vs. Quality in Kenya: Impact on Children from Low and High Income Households." In *Determinants of Educational Achievement and Attainment in Africa: Findings from Nine Case Studies,* ed. Ronald G. Ridker. Washington, D.C.: USAID Africa Bureau.

6. Institute International Research (IIR). 1997. *Girls' and Women's Education: A Status Report on USAID Initiatives.* Arlington, VA: IIR.
7. American Institutes of Research reports on the "Girls' Scholarship Strategy" and interviews with Mona Habib.
8. A curious aspect of this reform was that it occurred at the time Mali was becoming more democratic—an idea associated in many people's minds with freedom. Teachers, parents, and students often explained poor attendance and poor study habits on the fact that "they were now free to do whatever they wanted." (Author's observation.)
9. IIR, *Girls' and Women's Education*, p. 14.
10. Michael Kremer, Sylvia Moulin, David Myatt, and Robert Namunyu. 1997. "Textbooks, Class Size and Test Scores: Evidence from a Prospective Evaluation in Kenya." In *Determinants of Educational Achievement and Attainment in Africa: Findings from Nine Case Studies*, ed. Ronald G. Ridker. Washington, D.C.: USAID Africa Bureau.
11. IIR, *Girls' and Women's Education*. Annex.
12. Strategies for Advancing Girls' Education, a USAID-funded program implemented by the Academy for Educational Development.
13. Andrea Rugh. 2002. *Multisectoral Approaches in Advancing Girls' Education: Lessons Learned in Five Sage Countries.* Washington, D.C.: Academy for Educational Development.
14. Andrea Rugh. 2000. *Starting Now: Strategies for Helping Girls Complete Primary.* Washington, D.C.: Academy for Educational Development, pp. 120–136.
15. Andrea Rugh and Heather Bossert. 1998. *Involving Communities: Participation in the Delivery of Education Programs.* ABEL 2 Consortium, Washington, D.C.: Academy for Educational Development.
16. Esther Duflo. nd. *Experimental Data from India* (paper nondated and nonpaginated).
17. Richard Maclure, ed. 1997. *Overlooked and Undervalued: A Synthesis of ERNWACA Reviews on the State of Education Research in West and Central Africa.* USAID Africa Bureau.
18. Ibid., p. 20.
19. Sumra Suleman. 1997. "An Assessment of the Community Education Fund in Tanzania: Pretest Phase." In *Determinants*

of Educational Achievement and Attainment in Africa: Findings from Nine Case Studies, ed. Ronald G. Ridker. Washington, D.C.: USAID Africa Bureau.

20. These are the author's observations on a trip to set up a research design for evaluating the impact of literacy classes on women.
21. This was a CEDPA project supported by USAID; the main facilitator was Mona Habib.
22. Fergany, Farmaz, and Wissa, "Enrollment in Primary Education," p. 2.
23. Ibid., p. 3.
24. Esther Duflo in a nondated paper on research in India. See also Hanuschek who recommends focusing education inputs on learning, saying the same amount of resources can be used more efficiently with this approach.
25. In Mali, the community schools increased enrollments of girls 350 percent over five years. See IIR, *Girls' and Women's Education.*
26. Karin A. L. Hyde, Esme C. Kadzamira, Juliet C. Sichinga, Mike P. Chibwana, and Ronald Ridker. 1997. "An Evaluation of Village Based Schools in Mangochi Malawi" and Joshua Mushkin. 1997. "An Evaluation of Save the Children's Community Schools Project in Kolondieba, Mali." In *Determinants of Educational Achievement and Attainment in Africa: Findings from Nine Case Studies,* ed. Ronald G. Ridker. Washington, D.C.: USAID Africa Bureau. UNICEF supported the development of community schools in Egypt and Pakistan that were owned by communities rather than the government or donors. In Egypt in 1996 USAID supported more than 110 community schools with 3,000 students of which 70 percent were girls and was planning 1,000 more. These schools based on more child-centered approaches sometimes had difficulty preparing and getting children into the next stages of government schools where learning methods and goals differed.
27. Kremer, Moulin, Myatt, and Namunyu, "Textbooks, Class Size and Test Scores."
28. Duflo Esther, Pascaline Dupas, and Michael Kremer. 2009. "Additional Resources versus Organizational Changes in Education: Experimental Evidence from Kenya." Unpublished, http://econ-www.mit.edu/files/4286.

29. Note: Duflo says that the effect was different in Kenya from what she found in India—see above—because in Kenya the parents were empowered to take certain actions while in India parents were merely told about poor exam results and left to take their own initiatives.
30. Maclure, *Overlooked and Undervalued*, p. 34.
31. IIR, *Girls' and Women's Education*, p. 20.
32. Anne Case and Angus Deaton. 1997. "School Quality and Educational Outcomes in South Africa." In *Determinants of Educational Achievement and Attainment in Africa: Findings from Nine Case Studies* ed. Ronald G. Ridker. Washington, D.C.: USAID Africa Bureau.
33. For more details, see Andrea Rugh and Heather Bossert. 1998. *Involving Communities: Participation in the Delivery of Education Programs.* Washington, D.C.: Creative Associates, Inc. pp. 13–31.
34. IIR, *Girls' and Women's Education*, p. 15.
35. Rugh and Bossert, *Involving Communities*, pp. 101–119.
36. Joanne Capper. 1997. "An Evaluation of the Aga Khan Foundation's School Improvement Program in Kisumu, Kenya." In *Determinants of Educational Achievement and Attainment in Africa: Findings from Nine Case Studies,* ed. Ronald G. Ridker. Washington, D.C.: USAID Africa Bureau.
37. Andrea Bosch. 1997. *Interactive Radio Instruction: Twenty-Three Years of Improving Educational Quality.* Washington, D.C.: The World Bank.
38. Andrea Rugh. 2000. *Starting Now*, pp. 157–172.
39. Ibid.
40. IIR, *Girls' and Women's Education.*
41. Maclure, *Overlooked and Undervalued*, p. 23.
42. Manzoor Ahmed, Colette Chabbott, and Arun Joshi. 1993. *Primary Education for All: Learning from the BRAC Experience.* ABEL, Washington, D.C.: Academy for Educational Development.
43. Ibid. 1997, p. 22.
44. Howard Williams. 2001. *Multisectoral Strategies for Advancing Girls' Education: Principles and Practice.* Washington, D.C.: Academy for Educational Development.
45. IIR, *Girls' and Women's Education*, p. 17. For more details, see Rugh and Bossert, *Involving Communities.*

CHAPTER 3

1. Much of this section comes from the author's notes and materials that she gathered to write a technical report entitled "Starting Now: Strategies to help girls complete primary," 2000. SAGE Project. Washington, D.C.: Academy for Educational Development.
2. At the time "middle class" tended to be defined in terms of education status rather than income level. In fact "lower-class" skilled laborers often had higher incomes than "middle-class" bureaucrats. By the 1980s and 1990s, university graduates had more than filled government positions and the government was forced to delay appointments and eventually abandon the promise of government jobs. A disproportionate number of women took civil service jobs as they became available because of the shorter hours and because the poorer pay was more acceptable as a second family income.
3. However, classes still tend to be sex-segregated, especially in higher grades of primary and in secondary. Most universities are coed.
4. Small Koranic schools existed from a very early period all over the Arab World. And although foreigners often introduced the first modern schools based on European models, when these schools came under local control they often were influenced by the patterns of Islamic education. This model relied on authoritative sources and respected teachers, and the idea was to transfer knowledge with as little change as possible. Thus in the modern system there came to be a literal acceptance of textbook content, teacher authority, and devaluing of independent critical thinking.
5. From the 1970s on many of the seconded teachers were members of Egypt's Muslim Brotherhood thus not only helping to establish modern education abroad but incorporating more conservative Islam into those foreign schools.
6. "Flying classes" were one of these creative ways to accommodate children. As one class vacated its room for PE, another took its place and so on throughout the day. That allowed an extra class of students in every shift.
7. In some instances doctors were called in to determine the age of children, usually by looking at their teeth.

8. At the secondary level it was 21 percent girls compared to 33 percent of 13- to 18-year olds overall, and at the tertiary level 4 percent girls compared with 7.4 percent overall.
9. El-Sanabary (1989) credits urban/rural disparities in literacy to the concentration of facilities in urban areas, a "cultural lag" among rural parents, and the lack of perceived relevance to agricultural activities. Others suggested that educated mothers became role models for daughters, and were able to help them with homework, but there were not so many of these women in rural areas.
10. Comprising about 6 percent of students at the time of the USAID project but increasing rapidly.
11. Any official who could afford the cost sent his/her children to private schools, which was the case for most high officials in the MOE. Therefore they were not even aware as parents of what went on in the government schools.
12. Basic Education Development Project village school studies.
13. Parents often phrased the benefit of education to girls as making them "enlightened" or more literally "filling their lives with light." Frequently mentioned was that educated mothers helped children with homework.
14. Earlier rural girls would have been married by puberty, but as more and more children extended their education the age of marriage rose. And, especially in urban families a premium began to be put on educated women who could work and help support their families.
15. See the Population Council's study, "Transitions to Adulthood: A National Survey of Egyptian Adolescents." 1999. Dokki, Egypt: Regional Office for West Asia and North Africa.
16. Civil servants were the main group that received a modest pension.
17. The United States has spent an average of $2 billion a year in Egypt since 1979, more than half for military assistance. Since 1979 about $815 million per year was spent on infrastructure (*Washington Post,* March 6, 2011, A14).
18. Two other important activities initiated during this period were an Educational Management Information System (EMIS) to improve data collection and analysis and a study of the MOE's management system.

19. The UN concept of "Basic Education" attempted to extend compulsory education to two stages of schooling, usually to grade eight or nine, and urged the introduction of practical courses such as carpentry, electricity, home economics, et cetera.
20. This amount of time allotted for the 1979 Survey seems a luxury compared with the quick in and out of today's assessments.
21. These research bodies existed outside the MOE and the MOE was reluctant to let other groups study the state of education, partly because it feared criticism and partly because it didn't want donor funds diverted elsewhere.
22. These schools were too heavily resourced to provide appropriate models for the budget strapped school system.
23. Detailed recommendations were also made for each functional area of the educational system.
24. The team was influenced by the school designs of one-time Minister of Education Hassan Fathy that were inexpensive, comfortable, made of local materials, and could be made by local craftsmen. Egyptian officials, however, preferred "modern" concrete models even though they were more costly, uncomfortable in both hot and cold weather, and couldn't be maintained locally.
25. Usually the schools were built so they could be expanded to a second floor if necessary.
26. There was no local sense of ownership in the schools, which may have been one problem. They were brought in by the government and local people felt the costs of repair should be borne by the government. Often the materials used in the schools were costly in local terms and not the mud and brick and white wash villagers knew how to deal with. In any case the MOE reneged on its agreement to maintain the buildings.
27. By 1991, three-quarters of the new schools were overcrowded and roughly one-third had double shifts.
28. Girls' and Women's Education: A Status Report on USAID Initiatives (1997), produced by the IIR Consortium under contract No.: HNE-5848-C-00-6046-00 for the Girls' and Women's Education Activity, USAID, Office of WID, Bureau for Global Programs, Field Support and Research.
29. Andrea Rugh. 2000. *Starting Now: Strategies for Helping Girls Complete Primary*, SAGE Technical Paper No. 1, p. 147.

30. The gross enrollment ratios while not terribly reliable peaked in 1990/1, declined in 1991/2, and rose to 1990/1 levels again in the following year (1992/3) where the rates stood at 98 percent for boys and 85 percent for girls.
31. Two- and three-shift schools were becoming commonplace, sometimes using the same teacher to teach in two or more shifts. BEDP studies showed that multiple-shift schools produced about the same levels of learning as single-shift schools provided teachers only taught a single shift.
32. Scores on these secondary school exams determined what faculties in the university students could enter. The highest scores allowed students to enter medicine and engineering, and the lowest scores, education and agriculture.
33. Nader Fergany, Ilham Farmaz, and Christiane Wissa, "Enrollment in Primary Education and Cognitive Achievement in Egypt, Changes and Determinants." In *Determinants of Educational Achievement and Attainment in Africa: Findings from Nine Case Studies*, ed. Ronald G. Ridker. Institute for Policy Reform, Technical Paper No. 62. 1997. Washington, D.C.: Office of Sustainable Development, Bureau for Africa, USAID.
34. E. A. Hanushek and V. Lavy. 1994. *School Quality, Achievement Bias, and Dropout Behavior in Egypt.* Living Standards Measurement Study, Working Paper No. 107. Washington, D.C.: World Bank. According to Fergany a decline in the standard of living may have made it hard for parents to pay even the modest costs of schooling.
35. The middle and upper classes of Egyptian society looked with disdain at manual laborers, and these practical classes were expected to bring a greater respect for manual skills and dignity for those who worked with their hands.
36. The evaluation followed one cohort for four years between 1987/88 and 1990/91 and showed that in grade one there was no dropout (promotion was automatic), in grade two (when passing exams begin) one boy for every 1.6 girls dropped out, in grade three, one boy for every 1.6 girls, and in grade four, one girl for every 1.5 boys. So as the girls progressed through the system, their number of dropouts slowed and eventually became fewer than the boys. These figures suggest that "program quality" as defined by the ability to pass tests affects young girls more than boys,

perhaps as a result of parents being less inclined to push girls to continue. By the end of primary only the most "gifted" and "dedicated" were left.

37. At that time in the 1980s there was little actual evidence of how family factors affected school-going decisions. Many of these factors today are well-known and more nuanced, but at that time much of the conventional wisdom about these behaviors consisted of assumptions put forth by members of the educated classes living in urban areas.
38. Young children in particular were prevented from enrolling by distance, even though it was not such a big factor for older children. But given cutoff ages for enrolling in grade one, young children could not be kept home until they could manage the distances to school or they would be too old to enter.
39. Indeed researchers commented that school girls were recognizable by their manners and clean tidy appearances, compared to the appearance of non-school-going girls.
40. One example involved the extermination of weevils that harmed cotton crops. Children in school were taught that the modern way was to spray them with expensive chemicals while most farmers believed it was better to pick the weevils off the cotton. Later studies showed the farmers were right especially given Egypt's cheap labor force.
41. In Egypt however rather than solving the problems of the next generation, participation declined among poor urban and rural children by the 1990s and 2000s because of increasing costs of "required private lessons" to ensure children passed exams. Efforts have been made to address the issue but the problem has never been resolved entirely because of low teacher salaries and the government of Egypt's inability to increase so many salaries significantly.
42. The evidence was there but educators were so used to separating quality and quantity that they failed to understand the extent to which program quality however it might be defined could affect the participation of children, especially girls whose parents were less willing to help them continue if their exam scores were low.
43. Formative evaluations usually take place during a project by its staff to measure progress on such outcomes as student learning. The point is to make sure the inputs are having

the desired effect and if not to improve the inputs before it is too late. Summative evaluations, by contrast, evaluate impacts at the end of a project to make sure the project has achieved its intended outcome.

44. The reasons girls stay home must be addressed directly, as when schools provide day care for younger siblings so girls are free to study, or in certain situations providing economic incentives such as scholarships or food items.
45. The Egyptians were not always reliable informants however, since they were torn between wanting their system to look good and wanting it to look bad enough for the Americans to invest in reforms.
46. *Girls' and Women's Education: A Status Report on USAID Initiatives* 1997. IIR for USAID's Office of Women in Development.
47. This may be true in terms of "program quality" but it is not entirely true for "increasing opportunities" as when places are expanded for girls but not boys, or girls are provided with scholarships and not boys.
48. See Andrea Rugh. 2002. *Multisectoral Approaches in Advancing Girls' Education: Lessons Learned in Five Sage Countries.* Washington, D.C.: Academy of Educational Development.
49. This may be a good choice when recruitment of students needs a boost, but it has often been difficult to keep up a high level of community commitment without an infusion of funds. See Andrea Rugh and Heather Bossert. 1998. *Involving Communities: Participation in the Delivery of Education Programs.* ABEL 2. Washington, D.C.: Academy for Educational Development.
50. For more see Rugh, *Multisectoral Approaches in Advancing Girls' Education.*

CHAPTER 4

1. Pakistanembassy.ru/history.htm.
2. Cynical Pakistanis say the government will not provide quality education to the lower classes as long as most federal officials came from feudal classes that depend on illiterate agricultural workers.
3. This system was later discontinued because education officials claimed it was of poorer quality but the reason was

perhaps more that officials could not control the teachers in these schools as easily and they had to employ local "unqualified" imams to get their cooperation. The schools however served a number of children who otherwise would not have had the chance to learn "modern" subjects.

4. Between 2000 and 2007 somewhat better data showed that rates were still low at roughly 54 percent overall (with 60 percent for males and 40 percent for females) and there were much lower rates for both sexes in rural areas.
5. Yemen had the biggest gender gap according to the 1998 Population Action International report.
6. At the time these independent surveys were considered more reliable than census data.
7. The higher failure rates of girls was surprising given that in many countries, including those with similarly poor programs, girls often do better on state-sponsored tests. Anecdotally this lower achievement rate of girls was attributed to traditional expectations for girls in conservative areas of Pakistan, and the fact that girls performed more of the household tasks that often interfered with their attendance and studying.
8. Physical punishments were only abolished in 2010.
9. For example, BRIDGES studies showed teacher training in Pakistani institutes did little to increase the student learning scores, and later studies showed that teachers were unable to teach certain topics because they lacked knowledge of the concepts. In both cases the training institutes could not change the curriculum to address these deficiencies.
10. The list stressed proper teaching credentials, neat dress, discipline, polite behavior, and keeping to schedules.
11. Much of the information about the USAID role was supplied by Ann Van Dusen.
12. The researchers administered tests and performed multivariant analyses on the data.
13. Pakistani officials however were unwilling to contract consultants using their USAID resources, and extra funds had to be made available to hire consultants.
14. Before PED there were roughly 13,000 primary schools in NWFP, with 10,000 for boys and 3,000 for girls.
15. An independent study suggested the gender gap could be erased with comparable opportunities for girls and boys.

16. The IMDC director recruited young teachers to replace the older entrenched writers who she felt would be difficult to train. Primary teachers in the lower grades tended to be younger and more flexible, and also more knowledgeable about children's capabilities. The writers blossomed under her tutelage.
17. One such concept was the cardinal points. Participants said they would describe east "as being where the sun was." All day the director showed them how the sun moved across the sky but several still refused to change their minds because, as they said, "that is what we learned in school."
18. The learning objectives met usual international standards and for the most part conformed to objectives stated in Pakistani federal goals. Some of the federal objectives, however, were not used such as "learning how to communicate an idea by telephone" since most rural schools and homes did not have telephones.
19. The idea was to disseminate the experimental books broadly in hopes that their successes would interest other teachers and supervisors in the same districts. In the early stages each supervisor introduced the books to a limited number of teachers, and as time went by he or she would expand the number of local teachers involved.
20. One such example was the overlapping, repetitious data forms sent to schools that principals automatically filled in every year without question.
21. Virtually everyone interviewed said they had been easy to use, which made the evaluators feel that for some reason the school staff felt compelled to respond positively. These results are therefore suspect although in a certain way they were the equivalent of "signing off" on an innovation some must certainly have resisted.
22. Previously, in-service training covered topics trainers thought teachers needed to know, but which in fact did not help them much in their classrooms.
23. At the time they had been educated, girls could skip math and take other courses once they reached upper grades.
24. The tapes came from a successful IRI English program in Kenya. In that country the multiplicity of languages required that school children learn English quickly to cope with an instruction entirely in that language.

25. The Director of Primary Education in NWFP who was the key counterpart in PED was later prosecuted for taking funds during the program.
26. The establishment of the IMDC, the seconding of primary teachers to staff the IMDC, and even the furnishing of the building all happened despite his efforts to slow the process. He claimed, for example, that it took six months or more to requisition furnishings, but appeared only faintly amused when the consultant requisitioned furniture piecemeal from all the Directorate offices in a matter of days.
27. When complaints came in from district officials (probably because consultants were uncovering too many embarrassing problems like paper schools, missing supervisors, and nonexistent teachers), he began requiring that consultants obtain permission before going to the field. The formal exchanges of letters took weeks and with tight schedules for introducing and testing materials, the IMDC consultants and staff simply went ahead without permission. In situations like that the Director said nothing and moved on. It was not at all an ideal situation.
28. The cars that had been provided by USAID to transport supervisors to distance schools were instead used almost entirely for DEOs and other high officials. When IMDC staff appeared in their districts to conduct their activities, the DEOs let them use the cars that by that time had run out of gas and were immobile anyway. Before they left IMDC staff topped off their gas as a means of thanking them and ensuring use of the cars the next time they came.
29. Teachers said the class was necessary to spread the difficult first grade curriculum over two years. Children were supposed to be memorizing paragraphs of writing within a month or two of starting first grade.
30. Existing grade one books had one alphabet letter per page with a sample word using the letter and the three written forms of the letter. At the end of the alphabet pages children were given paragraphs to memorize. Only very good teachers took the time to make the transition between the two. In the new IMDC books the first grade materials were divided into a Kachi year taken up with learning the letters, colors, and pre-math concepts, and the second year of first

grade provided the transitional time for decoding words and eventually doing real reading and writing.

31. One consultant noted that although officials often stated unequivocally that all schools in Pakistan were sex-segregated, when she visited a girls' school she found a large number of boys in the lower classes. When she asked the principal about this, the woman seemed genuinely surprised that boys were enrolled. This example is not unusual. Often officials claimed something existed that didn't and seemed quite sincerely to believe it did. It was an ability to believe in things as they should happen rather than as they actually did, a tendency that was reflected in disbelief about the Kachi class, in east being wherever the sun was, and in the conviction that good teachers could be identified by characteristics of neatness and manners.
32. The data from these schools were analyzed in the IMDC rather than the EMIS.
33. This tends to be true for developing country school systems in many parts of the world. Without adequate measures of student learning it is difficult to know how these systems perform or whether they are improving.
34. The assumption was that teachers need a structure that channels them into new methods of teaching. Good teachers were free to deviate from the format as long as their students showed mastery of the skills.
35. The money had been obligated and halting the flow would have created a crisis in Pakistani-American relations.
36. Too late for PED the Brown amendment in 1995 exempted most forms of economic assistance from the Pressler amendment prohibitions.
37. Senior officials in one district found it difficult to believe children could learn through phonetic approaches because of what they believed was an inability to reason in the primary years. They also balked at starting the teaching with consonants sounds since previous texts had always started by teaching "a" first because that was how the Koran started.

CHAPTER 5

1. Mosque schools of course existed for much longer.
2. The institutions by that time included eight modern language schools, five for boys and three for girls.

3. A. Rasul Amin. 1987. "The Sovietization of Afghanistan." In *Afghanistan: The Great Game Revisited,* ed. Rosanne Klass, p. 313. New York: Freedom House.
4. "Afghanistan: The Geopolitical Implications of Soviet Control" by Elie Krakowski in *Afghanistan: The Great Game Revisited,* ed. Rosanne Klass. 1987, p. 175–176. In 1984 alone, for example, 834 seven- to nine-year olds were shipped to Soviet boarding schools for ten years of education. Older youths received scholarships for specialized training at higher levels of education.
5. This includes 36 faculty who were executed, 6 who were jailed, and 276 who fled. See Amin, *Afghanistan*, p. 319.
6. Ibid., p. 315.
7. Ibid., p. 322.
8. Roughly 85 percent are Sunnis and the rest Shi'is.
9. For example, schools funded by the Swedish Government operated virtually unhindered during the Taliban period.
10. A year later UNEO estimated that 3 million children in Afghanistan were between the ages of seven and thirteen, with 50 percent of the boys and 6 percent of the girls enrolled. They also estimated that 6 million lived abroad as refugees.
11. Afghans prefer the term "refugee villages" to "refugee camps."
12. Enrollment figures in 1995 are higher than in 1998 because girls were still in school, and because more families may have fled the country after 1996, as a result of the deteriorating conditions in the schools.
13. That number seems grossly underestimated if enrollments of 3 million after the US invasion are any indication.
14. According to Central Institute for Education Technology (CIET) statistics.
15. Mainly they removed images of people.
16. One exam given by an NGO for example asked the applicant among other items to tell the date of the Virgin Mary's birth. And the scores on the more skill-based math exams were so low that candidates with scores in the 20 percent range were hired as the most competent.
17. Technically the Taliban were making inroads in the south by 1994 but they did not take over Kabul until 1996.
18. Whatever the abuses of the Taliban, they were seen as creating greater stability and safety for local populations.

19. These issues are summarized from the UNICEF publication "Education for Afghans: A Strategy Paper" (July 1998).
20. ACBAR in theory was charged with approving projects to avoid overlap and lack of coordination. Unfortunately however, a number of international groups ignored them. There were branches in Peshawar and Kabul.
21. Visits to private homes were banned for foreigners so they had to be organized in secret, and MOE officials wouldn't see women so she accompanied the head of an international agency as his "delegation" to pay respects to the Deputy Minister.
22. The information was collected by an SC staff member, Hans Zomer.
23. These consisted of a complete set of detailed learning objectives such as "addition of 2 digit numbers" with examples. A member of a participating NGO organized a workshop around the Basic Competencies asking participants to identify objectives from their existing textbooks. The workshop failed for several reasons. Existing lessons were not organized around objectives and therefore it was virtually impossible to identify objectives. Participants as a consequence became confused about the Basic Competencies, thinking they were some kind of inferior textbook rather than a framework for developing books. This misunderstanding turned out to be a setback for the new approach when the convener of the workshop blamed the problem on the new materials and their developers.
24. One provider that didn't want to revise its program used BC as a framework for developing its own textbooks.
25. To avoid confusion the textbooks from this point on are called BC materials.
26. HBGS met three hours a day, five days a week, eleven months of the year, while RV schools met four hours a day, six days a week, for ten months.
27. The HBGS teachers were paid considerably less even when their qualifications matched teachers in RV schools.
28. RV schools enrolled six- to eight-year olds and not beyond. HBGS admitted girls from six to ten or when an RV school existed nearby, only girls older than the RV limit of eight years of age. NFE took females of all ages.
29. The scarcity of female teachers sometimes meant a trusted local male was recruited to teach girls or coed classes.

30. SC took over these schools after UNHCR failed in its efforts to turn over the schools to the refugee communities.
31. As in Pakistani and Afghan schools grade four was the point when the subject matter required specialist teachers.
32. The RV schools, being much larger, all had principals who oversaw their programs on a daily basis, and required far fewer supervisory visits from headquarters staff.
33. The exceptions were relatively new teachers who had not been fully trained.
34. They were transparent because students, teachers, and supervisors would know in advance the skills to be tested.
35. This title conveyed the idea that this was the first of a series of testings to determine whether future improvements actually led to better learning. Since existing textbooks were not organized around competencies this was in fact the first time a test of this kind was given. It assumed that children in any program would attain certain basic skills of reading, writing, comprehension, and math computation.
36. The Basic Competencies were the ones developed by Afghan educators as described in "Activity One." They were not systematically addressed in classroom teaching in the schools but as internationally accepted skills the children should have been learning them in an effective learning program.
37. The HBGS classes, which had been more recently established, at most had only completed the grade three level.
38. The consultant for the qualitative study had completed a study of HBGS classes only a few months earlier.
39. There were not enough RV-boys only schools to use as a category.
40. Classes in these schools were usually taught by men.
41. In BRIDGES' studies in Pakistan, the length of teachers' academic training had an impact on student scores.
42. It was difficult to find qualified female teachers so they were recruited from a wider radius than male teachers.
43. Posters with these objectives were later mounted on classroom walls by subject and grade level to remind RV and HBGS teachers what they should teach.
44. For example, a foreign staff member who believed in more child-centered approaches was not happy with an "exam-centered" approach, even though her Afghan staff seemed more inclined to accept the idea.

45. For example, where female teachers were not available older students with reading skills might be able to study in small groups or at home with self-instructional materials and a "roving teacher" who visited intermittently.
46. The school year in Afghanistan has two schedules, one starting in late March in areas with excessively cold winters, and one starting in September in areas with excessively hot summers. Having two schedules complicates school administration, and especially the holding of end of year exams.
47. The approach had been tested in NWFP and had also been validated in the qualitative studies of teaching-learning from the Harvard BRIDGES project in Pakistani rural classrooms that were similar to those in Afghanistan.
48. Despite UNICEF calls to include more Afghans, the roughly 50 Afghans invited were inundated by the more than 250 foreign experts who showed up at the conference.
49. Despite its warm welcome, the "Framework" was set aside, and the conferences became procedural forums to determine which donors would take leadership roles and how the development agenda would be shaped to ensure visible evidence of international donor support.
50. With the exception of a small "accelerated" program, formal schooling in Afghanistan was only provided when a building existed. The number of buildings that could be constructed was of course limited. Later buildings became visible targets for Taliban attacks.
51. The concern was that without recognition of equivalent credit, parents would be unwilling to support community schools and teachers would return to higher salaries in the formal system. This is indeed what happened.
52. The bulk of US funds, for example, was spent on building schools and printing Nebraska books. Many of these schools were poorly constructed, and fewer were actually built than were planned. As highly visible symbols of Western largesse, they were obvious targets for the Taliban.
53. UNICEF contracted virtually all the printing capacity of Pakistan to print the books, and a large UNICEF logistics team flew in from UN headquarters to set up an extensive field network to distribute the materials.
54. By 2010 the number of children in school increased to 8.3 million despite the still lack of security in many areas.

55. Presumably because of domestic politics in the United States.
56. Here official statements are summarized and paraphrased.
57. UNESCO works at the secondary and tertiary levels and specializes in the technical areas of curriculum development, planning, and worldwide monitoring. UNICEF does not have technical capacity in these areas.
58. Indeed, a member of the Taliban admired the final product when visiting UNICEF offices.
59. Some of the large donors however are members of its Board.
60. Some may have been reluctant to oppose the edict if they received some of their funding from the United States.
61. Some may have been permitted a reprieve for a limited time.
62. One of the early consultancies she organized was preparation of a resource guide of instructional materials, manipulatives, and reference reports that had been developed by the assistance community for Afghan education.
63. Pakistan is understandably wary of US assistance to the social sectors after being so easily abandoned earlier.

Chapter 6

1. Consulting companies seemed most concerned with pleasing donors and keeping within cost projections rather than with the rationales and premises of development. The COP's job was to make sure they were happy. In Egypt and Pakistan once the rough outlines of the project were defined and as long as reports were submitted regularly there was little interference by the donor, presumably because progress was roughly according to plan.
2. There are several common problems that have not been addressed because they did not occur in these projects: (1) sometimes contracts call for specific actions that hired consultants later determine are unnecessary or conversely that new activities need to be added to achieve results. Donor officers can take either of two routes: insist that the contract be fulfilled as agreed, or allow the contract to be amended. Good officers know how to "work the system" and make changes that will produce better results. Others can be adamant about sticking to the contract no matter how foolish that may be. (2) Sometimes the implementers

of projects are not the same as the designers of the project and this can lead to problems in the way activities are perceived and implemented. In these three cases the consultant worked on both the design and the implementation of the activities so the problem did not arise. Similarly, a design that promises more than it can deliver to win a contract can run into difficulty when consultants are brought on who rightly balk at operationalizing an unrealistic design.

3. Culture here refers to shared conceptual frameworks that help people make sense of the world. The BRIDGES studies in Pakistani classrooms for example suggested that direct styles of teaching-learning were more compatible with local respect hierarchies of age and authority than child-centered approaches that stressed a more equal status.
4. These unspoken goals assume graduates will be instilled with the "educated" characteristics admired by the society—in Pakistan, for example, being well-spoken, mannered, neat, and showing deference to authority.
5. For example, child-centered learning approaches (depending on how they were defined) and the development of critical thinking skills challenged conventional models and expectations that children would defer to authorities.
6. Comments of Mary Anderson. For more, see Luc Zandvliet and Mary B. Anderson. 2009. *Getting It Right: Making Corporate-Community Relations Work.* London: Greenleaf.
7. Literacy figures show access to education decades ago and not what is happening today. Foreign researchers often use the same proxies for quality and quantity mainly because there are no better data easily available.
8. As noted earlier, BRIDGES studies in Pakistan found that students tested on basic skills had no better learning results when taught by a trained or an untrained teacher.
9. The Paris Declaration, March 2, 2005, was signed by over one hundred ministers, heads of agencies, and other senior officials. The agreement committed countries and organizations to increase efforts to harmonize, align, and manage their assistance for more effective results. The document set monitorable actions and indicators including ones related to local ownership.
10. This is because the details of how to achieve the goals are not specified. Teachers for example can use any approach

they feel works to achieve the learning results: direct approaches, child-centered approaches, et cetera.

11. The goals are essentially universal—parents' desire for their children to learn so they can be productive, a universal expectation that children must acquire certain basic skills to be successful, and that an education system should be able to manage the process of schooling effectively.
12. In fact it is "expert" demands that the goal can only be achieved by applying certain approaches (whether rote or child-centered) that have been an impediment to progress. Belief in these approaches tends to rest on unfounded assumptions that because they work in the West they will work in the developing world. Perhaps worse, as expert advice, they discourage local communities from finding more appropriate approaches of their own.
13. Dambisa Moyo. 2009. *Dead Aid: Why Aid Is Not Working and How There Is a Better Way for Africa*. Vancouver, BC: Douglas and McIntyre.
14. Ibid., p. 145.
15. Ibid., p. 146.

References

Ahmed, Manzoor, Colette Chabbott, and Arun Joshi. 1993. *Primary Education for All: Learning from the BRAC Experience*. Washington, D.C.: Academy of Educational Development (AED).

Amin, A. Rasul. 1987. "The Sovietization of Afghanistan" (pp. 301–333). In *Afghanistan: The Great Game Revisited*, ed. Roseanne Klass. New York: Freedom House.

Anderson, Mary B., and Nuzhat Parveen Chaudhry. 1989. *The Impact of the Mosque School Policy on Girls' Access to Education in Pakistan*. BRIDGES Papers on Primary Education in Pakistan, Report No. 7. Cambridge, MA: Harvard Institute for International Development.

Ansary, Tamim. 2009. *Destiny Disrupted: A History of the World through Islamic Eyes*. New York: Public Affairs.

Banerjee, Abhijit, Rukmini Banerji, Esther Duflo, Rachel Glennerster, and Stuti Khemani. 2008. *Pitfalls of Participatory Programs: Evidence from a Randomized Evaluation in Education in India*. NBER Working Paper 14311. Cambridge, MA: National Bureau of Economic Research.

Bosch, Andrea. 1997. *Interactive Radio Instruction: Twenty-Three Years of Improving Educational Quality*. Washington, D.C.: The World Bank.

Capper, Joanne. 1997. "An Evaluation of the Aga Khan Foundation's School Improvement Program in Kisumu, Kenya." In *Determinants of Educational Achievement and Attainment in Africa: Findings from Nine Case Studies*, ed. Ronald G. Ridker. Washington, D.C.: USAID Africa Bureau.

Case, Anne, and Angus Deaton. 1997. "School Quality and Educational Outcomes in South Africa." In *Determinants of Educational Achievement and Attainment in Africa: Findings from Nine Case Studies*, ed. Ronald G. Ridker. Washington, D.C.: USAID Africa Bureau.

Coury, Diane, Susan Opper, and Judith Nahayo. 2008. "Early Child Development in Burundi: Community Delivery System (or community-driven response) to Improve the Well-Being of Young Children," unpublished manuscript.

Creative Associates International, Inc. 1991. *Final Evaluation of the Basic Education Project in Egypt.* Washington, D.C.: Creative Associates, Inc.

Deolalikar, Anil B. 1997. "Increasing School Quantity vs. Quality in Kenya: Impact on Children from Low and High Income Households." In *Determinants of Educational Achievement and Attainment in Africa: Findings from Nine Case Studies,* ed. Ronald G. Ridker. Washington, D.C.: USAID Africa Bureau.

Directorate of Primary Education. 1992a. *Kachi Study,* Peshawer, NWFP: Directorate of Primary Education.

———. 1992b. *Multi-Class Study,* Peshawer, NWFP: Directorate of Primary Education.

———. 1994. *Formative Evaluation Study of Kachi Materials Designed by the IMDC.* Peshawer, NWFP: Directorate of Primary Education.

———. n.d. *Teacher Content Knowledge Study.* Peshawer, NWFP: Directorate of Primary Education.

Duflo, Esther, Pascaline Dupas, and Michael Kremer. 2009. "Additional Resources versus Organizational Changes in Education: Experimental Evidence from Kenya," http://econ-www.mit.edu/files/4286.

El-Sanabary, Nagat M. 1974. "The Education of Women in the Arab States: Achievements and Problems (1950–1970)." Presentation at Middle East Studies Association. Boston, MA: Nov. 6–9, 1974.

Fergany, N., A. Amina, D. Al-Islambouly, I. Farmaz, S. el Sheneity, M. Mokhtar, and N. Ewais. 1994. *Survey of Access to Primary Education and Acquisition of Basic Literacy Scores in Three Governorates of Egypt.* Cairo: UNICEF.

Fergany, N., I. Farmaz, and Christine Wissa. 1996. *Enrollment in Primary Education and Cognitive Achievement in Egypt, Changes and Determinants.* Giza, Egypt: Almishkar Center for Research and Training.

Fergany, N., I. Farmaz, and Christiane Wissa 1997. "Enrollment in Primary Education and Cognitive Achievement in Egypt, Changes and Determinants." In *Determinants of Educational Achievement and Attainment in Africa: Findings from Nine*

Case Studies, ed. Ronald G. Ridker. Washington, D.C.: USAID Africa Bureau.

Filmer, Deon. 1999. *Educational Attainment and Enrollment Profiles: A Resource Book Based on Analysis of Demographic and Health Survey Data.* www.worldbank.org/research/projects/edattain/edattain.htm.

Floro, Maria, and Joyce Wolf. 1990. *The Economic and Social Impacts of Girls' Primary Education in Developing Countries.* ABEL Project. Washington, D.C.: Creative Associates, Inc.

Hanusheck, Eric A. 1994. *Making Schools Work: Improving Performance and Controlling Costs.* Washington, D.C.: Brookings Institution.

Hanusheck, Eric A., and Victor Lavy. 1994. *School Quality, Achievement Bias, and Dropout Behavior in Egypt.* Living Standards Measurement Study Working Paper, No. 107. Washington, D.C.: The World Bank.

Herz, Barbara, and Gene B. Sperling. 2004. *What Works in Girls' Education: Evidence and Policies from the Developing World.* New York: The Council on Foreign Relations.

Human Resources Management, Inc. 1979. *Basic Education in Egypt: Report of the Joint Egyptian-American Survey Team.* Washington, D.C.: Human Resources Management, Inc.

Hyde, Karin A. L., Esme C. Kadzamira, Juliet C. Sichinga, Mike P. Chibwana, and Ronald Ridker. 1997. "An Evaluation of Village Based Schools in Mangochi Malawi." In *Determinants of Educational Achievement and Attainment in Africa: Findings from Nine Case Studies,* ed. Ronald G. Ridker. Washington, D.C.: USAID Africa Bureau.

Ibrahim, Barbara, Sunny Sallam, Sahar El Tawila, Omaima El Gibaly, and Fikrat El Sahn. 2000. *Transitions to Adulthood: A National Survey of Egyptian Adolescents.* New York: The Population Council.

Institute of International Research. 1997. *Girls' and Women's Education: A Status Report on USAID Initiatives.* Arlington, VA. IIR Consortium for Office of Women in Development.

Khan, Jamsheeda, and Richard Cowell. 1991. *Primary Teachers in NWFP: Regulations and Practices which Govern Their Recruitment and Placement,* PED Program. Peshawer, Pakistan: Directorate of Primary Education, Government of Pakistan.

Khan, Sar B., and Ishtiaq Ahmad, n.d. *The Northwest Educational Assessment Program (NEAP) Report on Testing in NWFP*

Schools. Peshawer, Pakistan: Directorate of Primary Education, Government of Pakistan.

Khandkher, S., and Mark Pitt. 2003. "Subsidy to Promote Girls' Secondary Education: The Female Stipend Program in Bangladesh." World Bank, 2003.

Klass, Roseanne, ed. 1987. *Afghanistan: The Great Game Revisited*. New York: Freedom House.

Klitgaard, Robert. 1990. *Tropical Gangsters: One Man's Experience with Development and Decadence in Deepest Africa*. New York: Basic Books.

Kremer, Michael, Sylvia Moulin, David Myatt, and Robert Namunyu. 1997. "Textbooks, Class Size and Test Scores: Evidence from a Prospective Evaluation in Kenya." In *Determinants of Educational Achievement and Attainment in Africa: Findings from Nine Case Studies*, ed. Ronald G. Ridker. Washington, D.C.: USAID Africa Bureau.

Lewis, Maureen, and Marlaine Lockheed. 2006. *Inexcusable Absence: Why 60 Million Girls Still Aren't in School and What To Do about It*. Washington, D.C.: Center for Global Development.

Maclure, Richard, ed. 1997. *Overlooked and Undervalued: A Synthesis of ERNWACA Reviews on the State of Educational Research in West and Central Africa*. Support for Analysis and Research in Africa (SARA) project. Washington, D.C.: Academy for Educational Development.

Malka, Haim, and Jon B. Alterman. 2006. *Arab Reform and Foreign Aid: Lessons from Morocco*. Washington, D.C.: Center for Strategic and International Studies.

Morris, Timothy. 1991. *The Despairing Developer: Diary of an Aid Worker in the Middle East*. London and New York: I. B. Taurus.

Moulton, Jeanne, Karen Mundy, Michael Welmond, and James Williams. 2002. *Education Reforms in Sub-Saharan Africa: Paradise Lost?* Westport, CT: Greenwood Press.

Moyo, Dambisa. 2009. *Dead Aid: Why Aid Is Not Working and How There Is a Better Way for Africa*. Vancouver, BC: Douglas and McIntyre.

Mushkin, Joshua. 1997. "An Evaluation of Save the Children's Community Schools Project in Kolondieba, Mali." In *Determinants of Educational Achievement and Attainment in Africa: Findings from Nine Case Studies*, ed. Ronald G. Ridker. Washington, D.C.: USAID Africa Bureau.

Newsweek, March 14, 2011. The World Economic Forum's Gender Gap Index (2011), p. 50.

Office of Additional Director Primary Education. 1994. *Human Resource Survey: Teacher Supply and Distribution*. Quetta, Pakistan: Directorate of Primary Education.

Pakistan, Government of. 1992a. *Pakistan Integrated Household Survey Final Results, 1991*. Islamabad, Pakistan: Federal Bureau of Statistics.

———. 1992b. *Human Resource Survey: Northwest Frontier Province. Final Report*. Peshawer, Pakistan: Directorate of Primary Education.

Reimers, Fernando, and Donald P. Warwick. 1991. *The Impact of Schools on Achievement in Pakistan*. BRIDGES School Effectiveness Studies, Abstract 2. Cambridge, MA: Harvard Institute for International Development.

———. 1991. *Influences on Academic Achievement in Pakistan: Students, Teachers, and Classrooms*. BRIDGES School Effectiveness Studies, Abstract 4. Cambridge, MA: Harvard Institute for International Development.

Ridker, Ronald G. 1997. *Determinants of Educational Achievement and Attainment in Africa: Findings from Nine Case Studies*. Technical Paper No. 62. Washington, D.C.: USAID Africa Bureau.

Robinson, Wade M., Nadia Makary, and Andrea Rugh. 1987. *Fourth Annual Report of the Study of USAID Contributions to the Egyptian Basic Education Program*. Washington, D.C.: Creative Associates International, Inc.

Rugh, Andrea. 2002. *Multisectoral Approaches in Advancing Girls' Education: Lessons learned in Five Sage Countries*. Sage Project. Washington, D.C.: Academy for Educational Development.

———. 2000. *Starting Now: Strategies for Helping Girls Complete Primary*. Sage Technical Report No. 1. Washington, D.C.: Academy for Educational Development.

Rugh, Andrea, and Ahmed Nawaz Malak. 1990. *Connectedness: A Missing Concern in Education Systems: The Example of Curriculum Development in Pakistan*. Education Series, Development Discussion Paper No. 347. Cambridge, MA: Harvard Institute for International Development.

Rugh, Andrea, Ahmed Nawaz Malak, and R. A. Farooq. 1991. *Teaching Practices to Increase Student Achievement: Evidence from Pakistan*. BRIDGES Research Report Series, No. 8. Cambridge, MA: Harvard Institute for International Development.

Rugh, Andrea, and Heather Bossert. 1998. *Involving Communities: Participation in the Delivery of Education Programs.* ABEL 2. Washington, D.C.: Academy for Educational Development.

Steiner-Khamsi, Gita, and Carina Omoeva. 2009. *Access and Quality in Education: A Trade-Off.* New York: Teachers College, Columbia University.

Suleman, Sumra. 1997. "An Assessment of the Community Education Fund in Tanzania: Pretest Phase." In *Determinants of Educational Achievement and Attainment in Africa: Findings from Nine Case Studies,* ed. Ronald G. Ridker. Washington, D.C.: USAID Africa Bureau.

Toronto, James A. 1990. *An Organizational Analysis of the Ministry of Education, Arab Republic of Egypt: The Production Flow and Use of Information in the Decision Making Process.* BRIDGES Project Development Discussion Paper No. 346. Cambridge, MA: Harvard Institute for International Development.

UNESCO. 2010. *Reaching the Marginalized: Education for All Global Monitoring Report.* United Kingdom: Oxford Press.

UNICEF. 1998. *The State of the World's Children.* New York: UNICEF.

UNICEF and UNESCO. 2010. *All Children in School by 2015. Global Initiative on Out-of-School Children.* www.unicef.org/infobycountry/files/Final_OOSC_Flyer.pdf.

Van Dusen, Ann. 2008. *What Works in Expanding School Participation.* EPDC No. 08-07. Washington, D.C.: Academy for Educational Development.

Warwick, Donald P. 1991. *Who Completes Primary School in Pakistan?* BRIDGES School Effectiveness Studies, Abstract 3. Cambridge, MA: Harvard Institute for International Development.

Warwick, Donald P., and Fernando Reimers. 1991. *Good Schools and Poor Schools in Pakistan: How They Differ.* BRIDGES School Effectiveness Studies, Abstract 1. Cambridge, MA: Harvard Institute for International Development.

———. 1989. *Teacher Characteristics and Student Achievement in Math and Science.* BRIDGES Papers on Primary Education in Pakistan, Report No. 5. Cambridge, MA: Harvard Institute for International Development.

Warwick, Donald P., Huma Nauman, and Fernando Reimers. 1991. *Is Teacher Training in Pakistan Worth the Investment?*

BRIDGES School Effectiveness Studies, Abstract 5. Cambridge, MA: Harvard Institute for International Development.

Williams, Howard. 2001. *Multisectoral Strategies for Advancing Girls' Education: Principles and Practice.* Sage Project. Washington, D.C.: Academy for Educational Development.

Zandvliet, Luc, and Mary Anderson. 2009. *Getting It Right: Making Corporate-Community Relations Work.* London: Greenleaf.

Study Notes

In simulating the experiences of a development practitioner in as realistic a way as possible this book has explored how a variety of social, political, economic, and cultural factors and a range of actors (consultant, donor, education ministry, local authorities, teachers, parents) have affected both project outcomes *and* each other. The study questions below are a way for readers to reflect on the cases.

Class Discussion

The following questions are suitable for full class discussion. If we assume that individuals usually act in their own best interest, and that institutions and management systems governing schooling and donor assistance are designed to produce positive outcomes, why are so many aspects of these cases counterintuitive? For example,

- Why do some parents refuse to send their children to school—especially girls?
- Why do some educators and administrators refuse to adopt reforms that have proven in studies and/or practice to be effective?
- Why do administrators seem to focus on the least important aspects of teacher and student performance such as attendance, manners, or personal characteristics rather than learning?
- Why does the assistance community resist collaboration and insist on keeping its contributions separate?
- Why do donors mainly provide short- term rather than long-term financial commitments when behavioral changes of this magnitude take time?

The author of the case studies was a foreign consultant. She brought with her not only her training in anthropology and her understanding of the impact of education on individuals and communities but also the lessons she accumulated from each successive program. She was hired by a donor agency in each case, and was charged with providing her best advice on how to solve the problems identified by donors and host governments. She was, in all cases, working with a large team of external and local consultants, and these interpersonal relations played an important part in the eventual successes or failures of project activities.

- What part did the perspectives of the consultants play in the outcomes that occurred? Did they all agree on the approach?
- Did the consultants and local officials agree on the needs?
- What were the motivations of those involved in implementing the project activities? Were they the same for local officials and foreign consultants?
- Which aspects of planning and implementation were local educators involved in? Were they enough? How much did their involvement reflect the approaches used and the outcomes that resulted?
- What kinds of incentives appealed to the local participants? What kinds of incentives did the consultants offer? Were they enough? Might there have been something else offered to give them a greater sense of ownership?
- To what extent did "culture" affect the designs and outcomes of the project and the relationships of the participants?

In the case of Pakistan, most of the institutions needed to implement education reform were in place—schools, teacher training institutions, instructional materials development units, and testing systems. In Afghanistan, by contrast, the existing education infrastructure was in shambles. In Egypt, USAID was by far the largest donor to education, while in Afghanistan there were a wide variety of donors in the education field. In all three cases, reformers and resisters were found throughout the education system; in all three cases, the programs were slow to absorb the concerns of local communities. In all three cases, the programs attempted to address the three critical issues of girls' enrollments, poor learning, and lack of management capacity to deliver education.

- Why do you think the issues were so similar in all three cases?
- Were the proposed solutions similar, or were there important differences?

- How did differences in historical experiences with education affect the way officials in the three countries viewed education and the involvement of foreigners?
- Should communities have been involved? Might they have contributed to the outcomes? Would it be worth the resources to mobilize their support?
- What were the positive and negative consequences of having or not having a fully functioning bureaucracy?
- What could be the consequences if various donors and organizations don't coordinate their activities? What kinds of mechanisms might overcome this problem? How did the Afghan project try to overcome it?

Group Work

Role Playing

Each actor comes to education reform with a different perspective on what change is desirable or feasible and the outcomes that would be ideal. In thinking back to the cases, it is helpful to consider the mindset and perspectives of the participants, and how they responded to one another.

The reader should take one case and imagine himself or herself as one of the following:

- The minister of education;
- The representative of the donor agency in the capital city;
- The director of primary education in a province or district;
- The foreign consultant hired for his or her expertise;
- The principal of a school where the reform is taking place;
- A parent of a child in the school where the reform is taking place.

Some questions to consider are as follows:

- What limitations and sensitivities might surround your role as minister, donor representative, provincial director, expert, principal, or parent? How would you deal with them?
- What education problems would you want to address and what would be your priorities? What approaches would you propose?
- Can you anticipate what obstacles you might face? How would you overcome them?

- What outcomes would you want to achieve? What kind of evidence would satisfy you that your objectives had been achieved?
- What kinds of initiatives would you develop and who would be involved in developing them?
- What existing institutional structures would you use to implement reforms?
- How would you make sure the reforms are carried out and sustained?
- What arguments would you use to persuade others that your priorities and reforms are the best way to proceed?

These are important questions. If the minister of education defines success as increasing the number of children enrolled in school and the foreign consultant defines success as increasing the number of children who pass competency examinations, how does the project progress? If the donor gives priority to speed of implementation and local authorities focus on the visibility of the reforms, how can these two perspectives be reconciled? Even when the goal is agreed upon—say, increasing the number of female teachers in underserved areas or improving the relevance of the curriculum—the range of options for approaching the goal can be varied and constrained by the experiences, knowledge, and self-interest of the different actors. One cannot expect all consultants, or donors, or ministers of education to behave uniformly: consultants may disagree (and do) on goals and methods; and an education officer in a donor agency may approach education reform in a vastly different way from the director of the donor agency he/she represents. Try to determine the motivations and goals of the actors as they are presented in at least one of the case studies.

Assessing the Results

As was mentioned, there are some common themes in these case studies as well as some important differences. None of these programs was a total success; none was a total failure. Looking back over the three cases, and reflecting on examples of reforms described in Chapter 2, what approaches looked promising, and what did not.

- What are the major lessons you drew from these assistance efforts?

- What successes would you highlight in each case?
- What changes in project design or method of implementation might have improved project outcomes?
- What difference might it have made if the PED project in Pakistan had run its ten-year course rather than stopping after four years?
- What difference might it have made if the UNICEF BC textbooks had been used in Afghanistan rather than the Nebraska books?
- Would it have made a difference if parents had been consulted about the "practical" courses in Egypt before they were implemented? To what extent should the education program satisfy the needs of parents who may be illiterate, or should it meet international standards for primary level skills?
- Would it be better if innovations were tried in limited trials before introducing them to the entire school system?
- How would you monitor and evaluate the results of projects?

These are the types of questions that education experts, donors, school administrators, and government officials must ask themselves with each reform experience so they can improve their performance in the future. The answers are never easy nor without controversy.

ANALYSIS

Choose one of the case studies and prepare an analysis in writing by addressing the questions that follow:

- What are the major lessons you drew from the case?
- Could something have been done to improve the outcomes given the level of donor support and the receptivity of local officials?
- Are there other approaches to the issues in this country that might have been more effective under the circumstances at the time?
- Would you argue for international assistance or not in this case, knowing what you now know about the outcomes and international development in general?

Index